PUBLISHER'S ACKNOWLEDGEMENTS

Some of the people who helped bring this book to market include
the following:

Editorial and Production
VP Consumer and Technology Publishing Director: Michelle Leete
Associate Director–Book Content Management: Martin Tribe
Associate Publisher: Chris Webb
Publishing Assistant: Ellie Scott
Senior Project Editor: Sara Shlaer
Editorial Manager: Jodi Jensen
Editorial Assistant: Leslie Saxman

Marketing
Senior Marketing Manager: Louise Breinholt
Marketing Executive: Kate Parrett

Composition Services
Compositor: Wiley Indianapolis Composition Services
Proofreader: Linda Seifert
Indexer: Potomac Indexing, LLC

Cover design input from Andrea Austoni, `cutelittle`
`factory.com`

SMASHING

Successful Freelancing for Web Designers

THE BEST OF SMASHING MAGAZINE

Smashing Magazine

WILEY

A John Wiley and Sons, Ltd, Publication

This edition first published 2011
© 2011 Smashing Media GmbH

Registered office
John Wiley & Sons Ltd, The Atrium, Southern Gate, Chichester, West Sussex,
PO19 8SQ, United Kingdom

For details of our global editorial offices, for customer services and for information
about how to apply for permission to reuse the copyright material in this book
please see our website at www.wiley.com.

A catalogue record for this book is available from the British Library.

978-1-119-99273-8

Set in 9.5/11.5 Minion Pro by Wiley Indianapolis Composition Services

Printed in U.S. by CJK

Contents

Contents

Contents

Contents

PREFACE

Being a great web designer or developer is one thing. Running a successful freelance business is another. Whether you already have work experience in companies or you've just graduated from design school, being self-employed entails a number of tasks you most likely didn't have to deal with so far. As a freelance web designer you also have to be a project manager, office administrator, accountant, controller, and IT expert.

Juggling all of these often unpopular tasks while conceiving creative ideas and producing splendid websites can be very arduous. To help you with this feat we have compiled 21 selected articles about successful freelancing that were published on *Smashing Magazine* and *Noupe* in 2009 and 2010 (plus two all new articles). These pieces offer you invaluable tips and guidelines from professionals in web design. The focus lies on communicating with clients and co-workers, including marketing strategies and pitching, as this tends to be most problematic for freelance web designers.

We hope this book will make you even more successful and help you master your own "juggling."

— *Sven Lennartz, Vitaly Friedman, Manuela Müller*

BASIC SKILLS OF FREELANCE WEB DESIGNERS

1

ESSENTIAL HABITS OF AN EFFECTIVE PROFESSIONAL FREELANCER

by Rob Smith

THERE'S VERY LITTLE to stop anyone from becoming a freelancer. In a highly competitive and, in most places, saturated market, you need to make sure your reputation as a freelancer is well-managed and continues to grow. It's very possible to get a good reputation without being the best in the world, and it's even easier to lose that reputation. In this chapter, we explore 15 habits that are essential in helping freelancers effectively safeguard and grow their reputation, and we'll also discuss how to make freelancing work for you.

MARKETING AND RELATIONSHIPS

This first set of tips offers advice to help you attract and retain clients.

1. THE PRESENTATION HABIT

Your website should be at the center of your marketing strategy. It's where people go to see who you are, what you're about, whether you know what you're talking about, and what work you have done. It's your silent 24/7 salesman, and it needs to be right. Fortunately, what your website needs is straightforward:

- Well-presented work with a good description of the roles you played
- A brief history of who you are and why you're where you are
- Contact details that are easily accessible
- Content that is continually tweaked, added to, and updated

Other than that, you can go wherever you want with your own website — and so you should. Personality is key.

Jason Santa Maria (http://jasonsantamaria.com/) goes whole hog with a new design for each post — a lot of work but he stands out from the crowd as a result.

2. THE NETWORKING HABIT

They say that within 6 degrees of separation, everyone knows everyone. So you need to make sure that everyone within your 1st degree (i.e., people you know), know exactly what you do. It needs to be exact as well. If you're a developer you don't want people saying you're a website designer, and so on. Your current network of friends, family, and associates are your free word-of-mouth marketing, so get them talking about you right now.

Once this is done, your network needs to be extended and enhanced. Register with any social networking platforms that can work for you — LinkedIn, Facebook, and Twitter. Within those places, start getting into the right circles. On LinkedIn you may join some appropriate discussion groups that are either local or skill-based. On Twitter you may start tweeting and including appropriate hashtags so more people can see your tweet on that subject.

There are many ways to network and connect with people, so it's crucial that a freelancer not be afraid to talk to people and share information and contacts. Learn the networking habit and get yourself known.

3. THE NICHING HABIT

Freelancers can get into the habit of not only finding their niche, but creating niches. A niche in this case is an area in your overall field of work in which you particularly specialize. If you've become very good at creating websites for golf courses, for example, then that's a great niche.

The reasons for having a niche are simple: It's easier to become an expert in a niche. It's easier to sell to other prospects within that niche as they can see what you have done before. As an expert in that niche you can charge a premium for your depth of knowledge. The key to this habit is to proactively build your own niches. Seek out profitable areas in which you can work and concentrate on building niches.

4. THE PRICING HABIT

How you price your projects can easily be the difference between winning and not winning some work. Your pricing needs to be transparent at all times and should be agreed upon up front. Things go wrong when hidden costs appear later on. Clients like to know how much they're paying, when they're going to pay it, and what they're paying for. So make it clear from the start.

Second part of the pricing habit: protect yourself. It's easy to get so wrapped up in winning a project that you forgot some simple rules. If you have never worked with a client before, ask for a small percentage of the fee before you do any work. At this early stage, you won't know whether they will pay! Reduce your bad debt by either only working for clients you trust or having some remuneration first.

Third part of the pricing habit: be flexible. Make sure you find a way to make the commercial deal a win-win for both parties. This could be:

- Monthly payments (regular cash flow over the course of the project)
- Payment when you hit certain project milestones (e.g., project performance)
- Deposit and balance on completion (best avoided for cash flow reasons)
- Possible exchange of services

5. THE GROWTH HABIT

It's been claimed that it costs seven times as much in resources to acquire a new client than it does to grow an existing one. So the growth habit is about proactively looking at your clients in detail so you can discover new ways to help them.

One practical way to do this is to cross reference. Write all your services across the top of an Excel sheet, and then put your clients down the left hand column. Now place an X in the box where a service you have done matches a client. The boxes without Xs are potential growth opportunities and should all be explored before spending too much energy trying to acquire new clients.

BUSINESS AND TIME

These tips will help you manage your time and enhance your business reputation.

6. THE TIME MANAGEMENT HABIT

Lacking good habits in time management could cause you to overcommit yourself at certain times, which could lead to:

- Missing a deadline and disappointing a client
- Producing sloppy or inaccurate work
- Causing yourself stress because of the pressure to get everything done

The solution to this is an effective planning mechanism. Estimate how long the work will take you, and then add a buffer to your estimation. This will ensure that, if it does take longer, it won't eat into other projects. A 50% buffer works well. That may sound like a lot, but if you go over by 25% and then there are additional client emendations, you'll need it. Once you have the total time allocation, add it to your diary. Now, here's the crucial part: Do not move it, shrink it, or change it in any way. If you have to do something urgent that will interfere with that scheduled work, make sure the time is reallocated elsewhere.

A simple calendar application like Google calendar or Outlook can help you plan your time as a freelancer. If you struggle with where all that time goes and want to get serious about making improvements in time management, something like Rescue Time (www.rescuetime.com/) can really help.

7. THE FLEXIBILITY HABIT

Being flexible, responsive, and effective at what you do will allow you to handle unexpected situations, such as when a client contacts you with urgent needs and expects you to help. Having set aside time in advance for such urgent situations will ensure that you earn a reputation as a flexible worker.

What happens if nothing comes up to fill that pre-allocated time? Well, you might finish that other project early and can add something special. What happens if the whole day is taken up by an urgent project? No problem, you had already planned this might happen, so you won't let anyone down.

Of course you're not going to be able to foresee everything, but a certain level of flexibility will allow you to please your clients and be relatively free of stress because of time constraints.

8. THE HONESTY HABIT

Agencies will not use you again if you let a client down, and your chance of repeat work is slim to none. In the same way, you should not overcommit your time, but stay within your capabilities. We all need to stretch ourselves on new projects and learn new techniques and practices — that's not what this is about. This is about promising to do a task in a specified time when, in actuality, you don't have any idea whether it's feasible or not. Above all else, people appreciate honesty. You're better off being honest about whether you can handle a project rather than taking the risk of letting them down.

So how can you grow your skills and help your clients? By being honest and asking some good questions:

- "I don't think this project is right for me. I don't have much experience in [insert technology here]."
- "I can really help you with the [insert service here] part of this project, but I know another freelancer who can help with the [additional service]. Would you be happy if I managed the project for you but outsourced this other work?"
- "I'll need more information before I know how long this project will take. Would you mind if I spent a couple of hours doing some research so I can give you an accurate timescale?"

9. THE OVER-DELIVERY HABIT

Do not deliver your projects early. Sound strange? It's not. If you deliver early, there's a possibility the client will think you overcharged, and may expect part of his payment to be returned. They might also expect future work to be completed ahead of schedule, which may set a bad precedent.

Instead, use the extra time to focus on whizz-bang elements — those extra bits of polish and creativity that will gain you the reputation you deserve and let you grow. For a designer this might mean spending time adding nice touches to your graphics; for a developer, it could mean more time to implement a cool piece of JavaScript to replace the plain functionality you originally settled for. The "over-deliver" will earn you a solid reputation, whereas finishing early could get you into trouble.

10. THE BUSINESS ADVICE HABIT

Although as a freelancer you're skilled at what you do, don't assume you'll be able to do your accounts and bookkeeping, fill in tax returns, produce an invoice, or write a proposal all by yourself.

Seek regular advice from respected professionals to help you with these aspects of running your business. This might include speaking with people who run their own operations and understand the ins and outs better than you do. Learn as much as possible from their experiences and mistakes.

SPECIFIC BUSINESS AREAS

What's out there to help you run your business and what areas do you need to focus on? In this section, we discuss some applications that have earned reputations for helping freelancers do their jobs and be more professional.

11. THE EMAIL HABIT

Email is toxic. As a freelancer you can easily become what's commonly known as a busy fool. You might spend a significant part of your day just sending and receiving email without ever getting any work done. Instead, be in the habit of controlling email, and not letting it control you.

To do this you need to:

- Turn off all the little reminders, message counts, and other indicators that may catch your eye
- Configure your email client to run a "send and receive" at longer intervals, maybe as little as once per hour
- Set aside blocks of time in the day to deal with all email, and then switch it off; if something is urgent, people will use the phone
- Use the "touch it once" philosophy; fully read and deal with every email you open, instead of half-reading some and coming back to them later

12. THE PROJECT MANAGEMENT HABIT

Some clients will want you to fit in with their processes, while others will not enforce this. You need to have very clear processes for how you start working with a client and start a new project. What questions do you ask a new client? Where do you store the information they tell you? How do you keep track of how close the deadline is? Where do you store all the files they send you?

Email is not sufficient for this! Things will get lost, forgotten, or overlooked. You might prefer cardboard folders or ring binders or whatever works for you — but use something and stick to your own system. There are applications like Basecamp that can help with this.

Basecamp, one of the most popular web-based project management tools.

Source: www.basecamphq.com The names and logos for Basecamp, Highrise, Backpack, and 37signals are registered trademarks of 37signals, LLC. All text and design is copyright ©1999-2010 37signals, LLC. All rights reserved.

13. THE RESEARCH AND DEVELOPMENT HABIT

Sounds like a big company thing to do but R&D is essential to a good freelance operation. You need to be ahead of the curve or at the very least on it to be servicing your clients most effectively. Be in the habit of investing time for research and development. Expand your current skills and learn new ones. Never designed a billboard before? That's development.

Set aside time every week to do R&D. Build up a list of blogs that feed you new thinking and new ideas. Listen to informative podcasts. Read a thought-provoking book.

14. THE SALES AND CRM HABIT

How can you allocate your time and resources and figure out whether or not you need to be hunting for new work or concentrating on servicing current clients? You should know at any given time what your work pipeline looks like, how likely is it all to materialize, and at roughly what value.

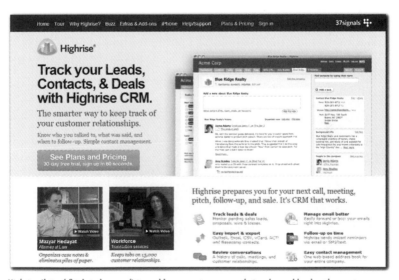

Highrise (http://highrisehq.com/) is used by many to manage their sales and leads at low cost.

15. THE ACCOUNTS HABIT

Making sure you have any easy way to produce, send, and track invoices is essential, as is getting into the habit of running your accounts professionally, because such habits will ensure regular cash flow. Applications like Blinksale, Freshbooks, or Simply Invoices can help formalize the accounts side of your business and give a good professional feel to how you operate. Clients will need invoices for their accounts — make sure they're not handwritten or unbranded.

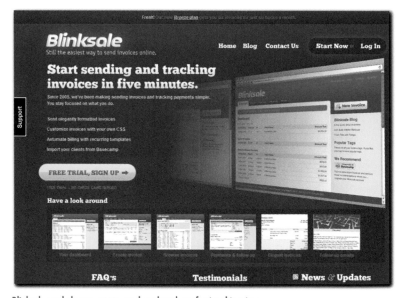

Blinksale can help you create, send, and track professional invoices.

Source: www.blinksale.com. © 2005-2010 Blinksale, Inc. All rights reserved. Blinksale is a registered trademark of Blinksale, Inc. Basecamp is a service mark of 37signals, LLC.

Rob Smith is Digital Director of Blueleaf (www.blue-leaf.co.uk/), helping clients with their digital needs from website to email marketing to analytics. He also writes in his own blog on digital media and e-commerce.

CHAPTER 2

COMMON QUESTIONS OF WEB DESIGNERS

by Andy Rutledge

THE DESIGN PROFESSION IS full of happy folks, and understanding why so many designers enjoy their work is not hard. But not all are so happy. If you're not careful, the joy of getting paid to pursue your passion can be tainted by the less joyous realities of the professional world. You see, no matter how skilled you are as a designer, unless you are equally prepared in professional matters, your prospects will be limited and your circumstances compromised. This is true whether you work freelance, for an agency, or in-house with a company.

Every week I hear from designers who are struggling to come to terms with these realities. Unhappy with their current circumstances, they write to ask for advice on improving their lot. Usually, they either claim not to understand how things got so bad, or they lay the blame somewhere other than at their own feet. In every case, however, the sole cause is their poor choices and lack of professional acumen. It needn't be so.

PROFESSIONAL DIAGNOSES AND SOLUTIONS

Here, I'll paraphrase a few emails I've received from designers seeking advice. For each, I'll diagnose the situation, explain in no uncertain terms what should have been done to avoid the situation and suggest a strategy the designer can follow to improve his or her circumstances.

These circumstances are not uncommon. Many of you reading this are likely experiencing similar problems… or may at some point in the future. I hope that the information, advice, and strategies presented here will help you avoid these and other problems.

1. GETTING STARTED AS A FREELANCE DESIGNER

Question: "I recently graduated from design school and have started freelancing, and I'm wondering how you get clients? How do you get your name out there?"

This person may just as well have jumped out of an airplane and then asked, "Now, how do I go about finding a parachute? Oh, and should I land somewhere specific? How exactly do I do that?" Even so, this lack of foresight is quite common. The immediate lesson is that you shouldn't become an independent professional with little to no professional experience, with no prospects, and knowing little to nothing about the business.

Fresh out of college or design school, you're not a professional; you're a technician (by definition, the opposite of professional). For the next few years you should be acquiring the skills, knowledge, and understanding required of a design professional. The place to do this is in the company of peers and under the wings of mentors: at an agency or in-house with a company. The successive lessons and built-in support system inherent in these environments are essential to a designer's professional development.

The way to "get your name out there" is to establish a pattern of excellent work and a reputation for integrity over several years, while you let your agency or company carry the burden of acquiring clients and running the projects. If you are any good, in time you will earn the respect of your peers and superiors, establish a good reputation (spread by word of mouth), and acquire professional acumen. If in that time you make any effort at all to share your work and thoughts with the wider design or business community, your name will become known (through word of mouth and your portfolio or blog), and your reputation will be built on substance rather than on social marketing's smoke and mirrors. This would be the appropriate time to embark on a freelance career.

As a freelancer, you'll be running the whole show. So, you've got to be an ace at finances and budgeting; at speaking with and converting potential clients; at knowing what to discuss in order to weed out unsuitable potential clients; at preparing all manner of legal and project-specific documents, writing proposals, project management, intra-project client communications (and being the confident, unflinching pro in the face of every client request, question, and distasteful situation); at dealing with dozens of types of unforeseen issues without hesitation; at maintaining tax information and constantly preparing various tax and business forms; at marketing, preparing, and maintaining your own branding and identity, with its various elements; and at knowing how to begin and conclude all kinds of projects confidently. Oh, and you'll also need a constant flow of interested potential clients. If you're not confident and accomplished in all of these areas, then you're not ready to be a freelance designer.

Freelancing is only suited to seasoned professionals. Pursuing a freelance career as your first step in the profession is almost always a foolish move. Professionalism is maintained by habit. If your first step is a misstep, you've set a poor tone for the work ahead. Unless you immediately correct your mistakes, the habits you'll develop will be clumsy and unprofessional.

15

2. HOW TO EXPLORE WHAT THE CUSTOMER WANTS

Question: "I'm not very good at the discovery meeting with clients. I'm never really sure what to ask or how to figure out what sort of design they're looking for. My project manager or CD usually ends up asking most of the design questions. What's the best way to handle this situation?"

This is a common issue for designers at agencies, especially those with little experience. Luckily, an agency is a good place to gain experience and competence. But the question signals a few issues that require attention.

First, design questions are not really appropriate during the discovery process. Granted, specific branding constraints may need to be defined and understood, but the design you will craft will come not from the client's judgment and understanding of design but from yours alone. The design will be your articulation of what they need, based mostly on their business aims, the website's purpose, their customers' needs and expectations, the end users' specifics, and so on. In fact, if you ask no design questions at all, you're probably on the right track.

Imagine for a moment that you're a physician trying to determine the best course of treatment for your patient. In that situation, you would not ask the patient what he thinks should be prescribed. Instead you would inquire about his symptoms, history, environment, physical needs (e.g., is he a pro athlete, or does he simply need to be able to get around normally?). The answers to these questions will define the constraints and indicate the appropriate course of action. Your patient's opinion on what prescription would be appropriate is likely irrelevant; he came to you because he lacks the ability to help himself.

Go into the discovery meeting prepared. Before the meeting, learn as much as you can about the company, its history, and its past and current activities. Script a list of questions — some specific to this client and some appropriate for any client — to get the ball rolling. These questions will serve as a springboard to more in-depth discussion, which in turn will flesh out what you need to know.

One more thing: you're the design professional and it's your responsibility to conduct the project successfully. You (not the PM or CD) should be driving the discovery. Use your time at the agency to improve your discovery skills, taking on more responsibility with each successive client. Reflect on each project's discovery process, and look for ways to improve the process and your questions. With time and effort, you should become competent in this essential part of the design process.

3. CHARGING COMPS: WHAT IS THE USUAL NUMBER?

Question: "Some of my clients expect three or four or even more comprehensive layouts (comps) from me. That's a lot of work, and I would prefer to show just a couple. Should I just charge more if they want more comps? How do some designers get away with just one or two for all of their clients?"

These are interesting questions, and they beg a couple more:

- Why is this designer allowing his clients, who are not designers, to set the number of design comps?
- Why is he letting quantitative preference rather than qualitative necessity frame his understanding of the issue?

Good design is not found by picking from a pack of arbitrary options, but is rather the result of deliberate, contextual choices. Taking a scattershot approach to design is in no way effective. Your clients may not appreciate this, but you certainly should! Your responsibility is to ensure that your clients don't shoot themselves in the foot.

The only person who knows how many design options are appropriate is you: the designer who is engaged in the process. And in almost every case there is one best design solution. Sometimes another compelling direction is worth considering and presenting to the client, but this cannot be known until you have fully engaged in the process, conscious of the parameters specific to that project.

In most cases, you'll explore a host of options during the design process. A thorough exploration will cull a majority of the trials, leaving only the most appropriate and compelling candidate(s) — one or two. These and only these design options should be shown to the client. Inferior designs should never be presented, even to fulfill a request for more options (options for what — mediocrity?).

As a freelance design professional, or even as an agency designer, your responsibility is to define how many design options to present in a given situation. If a potential client insists on a less effective and less professional process, do not agree to work with that client. Compromise never brings excellence and has no place in design or professionalism. If you become comfortable making this sort of compromise, other compromises will also become easy for you. Your clients deserve and are paying for more than a compromised design.

4. DRIVING THE DESIGN PROCESS IN AN AGENCY

Question: "I seldom get to meet my clients before I present design comps to them. By that point, the projects almost always become a tiresome series of re-workings of my original ideas. How can I change this?"

One wonders what these original ideas were based on if the designer has never met the clients. If so, either 1) this person is at the wrong agency, and/or 2) this person lacks the professional understanding or the backbone to insist on being the one to decide how the agency should structure design projects and client-designer interaction.

Relationships are built on trust, and trust is born of experience and understanding. Your client cannot trust someone they have never met and whom they know nothing about. So, when designs are presented by someone the client has never met, no wonder the client is a bit reticent and inclined to second-guess the designer's decisions. These and the ensuing problems are all a result of the designer's failings. Yes, it's on you. Always.

As the designer and an aspiring professional, you must insist on driving the design process. This means that you must be the one to meet with the client in the beginning. If a project brief is required, you must be the one to create it, based on your direct conversations with the client and his team.

If your agency has a process in place that prevents you from fulfilling your responsibilities, your options are either to change the process or to find a better agency. Anything less relegates you to an irresponsible practice in an unprofessional environment. Hopefully, this is not acceptable to you, because it would erode the habits you are professionally obliged to cultivate.

5. ASSESSING AND IMPROVING COMMUNICATION SKILLS

Question: "I love to design, and I think I'm pretty good at it. But I'm not comfortable talking to clients. Whenever I'm on the phone or in front of a client, I get very nervous. I think my nervousness makes me seem less capable, and I'm pretty sure I lose some of my client's confidence. What can I do to correct this? Should someone else do the talking?"

Effective communication is one of a designer's most important jobs. Every communication, whether by email or phone or in person, is an opportunity to demonstrate value and win confidence. And if you don't demonstrate value, you'll seldom win confidence. Like in one of the examples above, you may simply not be prepared to be a freelance professional.

If you fail in communicating, no matter how skilled a designer you are, you won't get the chance to ply your skills very often, and seldom for the best clients. The best clients are those who invest complete trust in their designers. That trust must be earned before any actual designing happens (see item 4).

And no, someone else should not do the talking. The design professional's job is to show confidence when dealing with clients. No one else can communicate your value or win trust for you. The reason clients distrust those who do not communicate with confidence is because this trait signals other incompetencies. This may sound harsh, but it's a fact: if you're not confident, it is because you lack capability (whether professional competence, design skill, or perhaps vocabulary) . . . and you know it. Address this void, and your confidence will shine through.

If you lack confidence in conversation, start to address this deficiency immediately or find another calling. Otherwise, you may have a bright future as a production artist somewhere, but not much of one as a design professional. Design professionals are experts at every aspect of interacting with people.

Confidence aside, it goes without saying that excellent vocabulary is an important component of effective communication. People judge you by your words, as well they should. Knowing this, your professional responsibility is to work on your vocabulary, just as you work on your design ability: daily.

BEYOND DESIGN: ASPECTS OF PROFESSIONALISM

Skill in design is only part of what defines a competent professional. Professionalism is also measured by integrity, preparedness in handling and interacting with clients, and breadth of understanding in the myriad of issues that will confront you in the course of working with others (whether clients, co-workers, employees, or others). Professionalism is also measured by how well you uphold ethical standards in making the difficult decisions in every area of your work.

Talent and skill can make you a technician; and a technician is, as we noted, not a professional. For context, think of traditional professions: lawyers, doctors, architects. The enormous responsibility they are entrusted with, and their ability to carry out that responsibility across the scope of their work, makes these people professionals. Thus, an able professional would not be troubled by the questions posed in this article. Rather, they would know precisely how to proceed or how to circumvent these issues. If you have any of these questions, you may not be prepared to be a design professional.

All of these situations result from designers believing that being a good designer is good enough. This profession has little room for those who lack a professional's integrity and broad understanding. Designers who are willing to compromise and simply accept the faulty decisions that are handed to them have had their profession stolen from them. These designers have no business working with clients who pay good money for professional service.

Be better than this. Your first step to success is to assume your rightful responsibility for everything that involves you. Dissatisfied with the flawed structure at your agency? You chose to work there; change your circumstances. Frustrated by your perpetual lack of prospects and stalled reputation? Sounds like you've got deficiencies to address. Overwhelmed by the challenges and complexities inherent in freelancing? You probably started freelancing without sufficient preparation.

Fix it. You fix it. It's all on you.

Designers: you get paid to do what you love. How great is that!? But this fortunate and enviable situation leads to fulfillment only if you take full ownership of your profession. Otherwise, you're carrying a time bomb. When it goes off, your career will either falter or be blown to smithereens. Don't let this happen to you. Educate yourself. Have the courage and integrity to habitually make good choices so that you enjoy a long and happy career as a design professional.

*Andy Rutledge is Principal at Unit Interactive in Plano, Texas. When not working, road cycling, or banging on the piano, he's usually found ranting about design or professionalism on his personal site, Design View (*www.andyrutledge.com/*).*

3 THE DESIGNER WHO DELIVERS

by Aurimas Adomavicius

WHETHER YOU DESIGN and code websites all by yourself or run a small business with a pool of talent, you will always face the challenge of how much to work on a design and UI before passing the mock-ups on to the developer. Moreover, how much visual work needs to be done in order to effectively present a website to a client? In this chapter, we talk about best practices for clear communication, which tools to use, and how to manage resources on both small and large projects.

THE APPROPRIATE NUMBER OF MOCK-UPS TO DELIVER

As the owner of a small business, I have watched our company grow from a part-time, basement-dwelling, under-the-radar operation to a small business with an office, chairs, desks, and staplers (aren't staplers an indication of legitimacy?). During this process of breaking out of our egg shell, we have birthed a company culture and a set of best practices, and we have gained valuable experience in the field of Web design and development. One of these nuggets of experience is acquiring the ability to save time and money by creating just the right amount of visual material to communicate clearly with both the client and website developer.

I won't even bother asking whether you've ever been assigned to create a custom Web application with an intricate UI, only to see your client pretty well freak out and tell you that it's completely the opposite of what they had in mind. And let's be honest: they freaked out not because they're Web infants who drool every time a Flash intro pops up, but because you failed to communicate the project and its functionality.

Don't get me wrong. Your UI was probably slick. It ran fast, the scripts were minified, it had sprites for all button and UI elements. From a technical and design standpoint, it was as hot as the BMW Mini Cooper back in 2007. The only problem was that your client was looking for a pickup truck.

Our approach to Web design and number of mock-ups is usually based on the size of the project. For the purpose of this article, I'll break projects into two categories: the brochure website (i.e., a content-oriented website about a company or individual), and the application website.

BROCHURE WEBSITE

For small websites, I recommend you sit down with the client and spend a good hour just learning about their business. Before this meeting, all you probably had to start with was an email from your cousin saying something like, "Listen, Mike over at Gadget Inc. wants a cool site that will be #1 on Google." After your meeting, though, you will be amazed at the quantity of relevant information that your client shares with you. Don't be afraid to ask questions: information that would normally be difficult to extract is but a question away when you're sitting face to face. Your inquisitive attitude will also reassure the client because it indicates that you're genuinely interested in solving his business problems.

Now that you have a wealth of information, you should be able to deduce what the client really wants (it might not be exactly what you originally thought). Make sure you understand well what websites they like and the reasons they like them, along with the colors, logo, and other visual cues that might help you get started on the design. If your client has not yet committed to you and is waiting for a proposal, you may want to provide a single mock-up with your proposal. A mock-up is often a worthwhile investment on a larger project, because it creates an emotional attachment with the client and speeds up the bidding process.

This more or less sums it up for small websites: clear communication with the client helps you establish a good base to work from, and the number of mock-ups should be kept to a minimum if you're good at listening. In case you get stuck on a minute detail that the client doesn't like, you could always post your mock-up on ConceptFeedback (`www.conceptfeedback.com/`) and get some feedback from other designers. Most of the time, peer opinion will sway the client to your side if you know what you're doing.

APPLICATION WEBSITE

Larger projects and web applications are a completely different beast and should be dealt with accordingly. Your requirements for the project will arrive as a request for proposal (RFP), sealed in a gold-encrusted money-scented envelope and put together by a project lead. A committee of people will be responsible for the content, functionality, and goals of the website,

23

and their opinions will be slightly different. The job of the designer and/or team leader will be to interpret the client's requirements and communicate them visually to the development team.

I have learned that written technical specifications are only as good as the people who read them. Your developers will understand them, but your client committee will interpret them in as many ways as there are people on the committee. Your responsibility, then, is to illustrate the project for both teams. All of the items mentioned above for the small website still apply, but you will also need to build an information architecture map, functional flow, interaction mock-ups, and more. As you're working through these visual elements, consider using some of the tools available on the Web to get feedback from a wider audience.

While mock-ups that encompass detailed functionality are a costly venture, they are simply the best thing you can do before writing a line of code, because an illustration will give your client the right expectations. As a Web development company, you would also be fortunate to have Web designers who understand mark-up, AJAX limitations, accessibility and readability implications, and more. We have had some curious interactions with designers who made fantastic brochures but couldn't mock-up a single screen of a website UI.

This approach, while time-consuming at first, will save hundreds of development hours, because the application will behave and look the way the client expects. Your information hierarchy and functionality mock-ups will allow your developer to work completely independently from the designer, with minimal interruption and questions.

RED FLAGS

Even if you follow these guidelines and wield a creative stylus, you will have conversations or get emails that should set off alarms in your head. These communications usually start with, "This is not as hip as I wanted," or "I was expecting something unexpected," or "We really want it to look social." These statements are problematic for a couple of reasons, the first being that you have a limited budget and time frame for the project and have already used up some of them. The second problem is that these statements are as clear as mud.

Well, just as with the requirement-gathering phase, your focus here should be to drill to the heart of these statements and figure out what exactly is meant by each. The work you have already done can usually be salvaged, and the client might want nothing more than a different illustration, color combination, or font stack. I suggest approaching this with changes that require little effort. Start with small tweaks, and then send the mock-ups. Continue with moderately complex changes, and then send the mock-ups. Rinse and repeat. What you will likely find through these small adjustments and your communications is that the negativity in their initial email was actually an exaggeration of a small issue.

LESSONS LEARNED

The route you take in a successful project will depend on the size and composition of your team and your ability to communicate with the client. The more projects our team completes, the more strongly we believe in visual communication, which falls strictly on the designer's shoulders. It is also safe to say that a Web designer is a mixed and intricate breed of professional: an individual who must understand business, be able to read customers, stay creative and fresh with visual solutions, and be technical enough to understand Web technology limitations and best practices.

Aurimas Adomavicius is the creative lead at DevBridge, a Chicago-based web application development company. He is also responsible for the creation of the website review community Concept Feedback. A photographer, web developer, and web designer, his opinion can be often heard on the company blog and on Twitter.

25

4

CRITICAL MISTAKES FREELANCERS MAKE

by Robert Bowen

SEEING AS WE are all human (well, presumably whoever is reading this anyway), we should recognize that mistakes happen. They even have that saying, "To err is human . . .," which goes to show that it is not only commonplace for us to err once or twice: it is *expected*. But a method is behind this madness, because making mistakes is one of the major ways we learn. This is no different for freelancers.

Finding our way over these bumps in the road often gives us valuable insight to take away. It helps us develop techniques and methods that we can incorporate into our creative process. As freelancers, we have the benefit of access to an entire online community that is willing to share its experiences so that we can learn without having to make the same mistakes.

So in this chapter, we look at some critical mistakes freelancers make. Hopefully, if you haven't already made one of these mistakes yourself, you can learn the lesson behind it.

THEY DON'T USE A CONTRACT

One of the first things freelancers learn when contracting out their services to others is . . . to use a contract! Unfortunately, we often learn this lesson the hard way. For whatever reason, we think that a particular client is someone we can work for without the aid and protection of a contract. This tends to end in one way: by biting us in the back end.

Without this safeguard in place, you open yourself up to so many potential problems, and you may inadvertently end up committing to more than you had intended or even imagined. Freelancers only make this mistake once, if at all. This lesson is not a secret in the freelance community. The advice comes up often: always use a contract. And many heed the warning once they hear it.

THEY MISUSE SOCIAL MEDIA (OR DON'T USE IT AT ALL)

Another common, but critical, pitfall that freelancers tumble into is misusing social media, if they even use it at all. Social media is a major tool that offers all freelancers an invaluable resource at their fingertips. An entire community of professionals connected via modems, ready and willing to offer each other whatever assistance they can. Neglecting this stream of industry insight, or not using it properly, can hinder the growth of your business.

Social media is about interacting with people and fostering relationships, which, if done with consideration and attention, can create opportunities you would have otherwise missed out on (not to mention friendships that can outlast jobs). Especially at the beginning of your freelancing career, if you make the mistake of misusing the media, you could be seen as an anti-social pariah in your corner of the Web.

THEY PUT QUANTITY OVER QUALITY IN THEIR PORTFOLIO

When putting their portfolio together, some freelancers mistakenly believe that the more they add to their portfolio, the better. Then it becomes about quantity and not quality of work. They forget the value of the portfolio in opening doors and creating opportunities.

The phrase "Put your best foot forward" applies in this situation. Your portfolio speaks volumes about your skills, freeing you from having to say too much and risk coming off as more arrogant than confident. Let your portfolio do the talking, and don't make the mistake of prioritizing quantity and sending the wrong message. Quality makes the best first impression, so make the most of it.

THEY STOP LEARNING

This one has to be said. It can do so much harm to freelancers, no matter what their field: that is, they stop learning. But especially for freelancers who work in a field as dynamic and ever-expanding as design and development, staying ahead of the curve is absolutely crucial to meeting your clients' needs.

This field is continually evolving with new techniques and applications. Throwing in the towel on education is virtual suicide. You, your work, and your career would stagnate. Thankfully, with this online culture we have today, cultivating an environment in which we can sustain our education is easy. Not taking advantage of these learning opportunities is a mistake that could potentially cost you your business.

THEY DON'T KNOW HOW TO DEAL WITH CLIENTS

Another common mistake is that freelancers forget their people skills when dealing with clients. For whatever reason, we let slip in our minds that clients hire us because they don't know how to do the work themselves. They are in unknown territory, and as freelancers we should always be sensitive to that and bridge as many gaps in knowledge as we can. This will only improve your future dealings with the client and earn you more respect and trust in the business.

Obviously, without clients, you are a freelancer in title alone, so make sure you know not only how to engage clients but how to entice them back. Being able to assess needs that they aren't even able to articulate and then communicating it all back to them is an invaluable skill. Neglecting it can be costly.

THEY FAIL TO PREPARE FOR DRY SPELLS

This mistake, failing to prepare for occasions when no work is coming in, is definitely better learned second-hand. Droughts hit even the best of us, especially in these tough economic times. Freelancers often forget to account for that in their pricing structure and to save up in good times for when things go south.

There is a logic behind the rates we charge, and part of it is to sustain us after we have completed work for one client and eagerly await the next. Of course, we can always find work to do, but paying work is what sustains us as freelancers. Calling this mistake costly is too close to punning for comfort, but its impact is definitely painful and could force you to suspend freelancing and seek out supplemental employment, thus making it even harder for you to create your own opportunities.

THEY OVERLOAD THEIR PLATE

This next mistake sometimes results from a fear of the aforementioned dry spell. Of course, greed might also play a role. Whatever the reason, some freelancers don't know when enough is enough, and they continue to take on new projects as their plate overloads. Overextending yourself and your business like this can destabilize your workflow.

Freelancers need a certain degree of self-awareness to know when they have reached their limit. Reputation — that is, a good one — is important to your business's development. Spreading yourself too thin is never good, and the distraction could hamper your creativity. This is another of those mistakes that are difficult to recover from.

THEY MISS A DEADLINE (AND THINK IT'S NO BIG DEAL)

This, too, is often a consequence of the previous mistake in our list. Falling behind when you are overloaded is all too easy, but missing a deadline can have a debilitating effect on your business. And if you think missing a deadline is no big deal, your career may be over before it begins. Deadlines keep you on track and help you multitask, as well as keep your client on track with the development of their project.

Once again, reputation is critical to building your brand and making your mark in the freelancing market. And a great way to ruin that reputation is by proving yourself unreliable. Stay productive and ahead of your tasks to avoid disrupting your client's timetable. If you end up making this mistake, own up to it. Don't offer excuses, simply propose a new timetable and continue working hard to meet it. But clearly acknowledge the problem you have created for your client. If you make this mistake once, you may not have an opportunity to make it again.

THEY LACK CONFIDENCE

Lacking confidence in themselves or in their work is another mistake that can plague freelancers, even beyond their business. Being your own worst critic and holding your work to a higher standard than that of others is natural (right?). But at a certain point, you are no longer critiquing so much as tearing down your work. Dismissing the talent and abilities that have carried you this far is misguided and will do nothing for your productivity.

Without confidence, making it as a freelancer will be extremely difficult. You'll start taking useful and well-intended criticism bitterly, missing the person's point and spiraling further into a pool of doubt and self-pity. Lack of confidence hinders your skills and the growth of your business. Clients will pick up on it quickly, because the freelancer is supposed to have a commanding role. Our responsibility is to guide the client to make effective decisions and win them over to our point of view; without confidence, this becomes unlikely. You'll undervalue both yourself and your work. So have faith in your abilities, and know that your unique voice is needed in the ranks of the freelancing arena.

THEY GO TO WORK FOR SOMEONE ELSE

Another blunder freelancers make is to work tirelessly to build their business, only to accept the first offer for a cushy job that comes along. No longer being your own boss would seem easy to adjust to, but it can be like moving back under your parents' roof after you've tasted the freedom of living on your own. It simply doesn't fit as comfortably as it once did. Simply readjusting is not so easy because freelancing is more than a job: it is a way of life.

Some people tell themselves that freelancing was all along a stopgap to some greater dream, but true freelancers find that pill hard to swallow. For some, that might be true, but then those people were not freelancers so much as temporary independent contractors. Freelancers crave the freedom that comes with the 'lancing. Still others believe they can work for someone else and maintain their freelancing on the side. In theory, this might appear viable. The reality is harsher: freelancing is full-time. It is a way of life, and turning it into a part-time job spells trouble.

Robert Bowen is an emerging author, celebrated podcaster, and poet. He is the co-founder and imaginative co-contributor of the creative design and blogging duo at the Arbenting Blog and Dead Wings Designs.

5

THE IMPORTANCE OF CUSTOMER SERVICE

by Robert Bowen

ONCE UPON A time, when the Internet was dialed-up and 36,600 KBPS was like lightning, I was living in a small town working for a computer retailer and Internet service provider. My boss at the time was . . . well, let's just say that customer service was not his priority. Not only would he berate and verbally assault almost every customer who happened to cross his path when he was frustrated by a computer repair, but his relentless tirades caused customers to leave either in tears or on the verge of them.

I wondered during my four-year stint, attempting to clean up the customer service messes he left in his wake, how he managed to stay in business in the years before and since my employment. And the answer was simple: he was a big fish in a tiny pond.

In a town of 18,000 residents, there were only three computer retailers that had qualified technicians who could handle in-house repairs. He was one of them. But as web freelancers, we are swimming in an ocean that is teeming with qualified fish, all waiting for a hook from clients. So, we have to pay special attention to the customer-relations part of our business if we want to build and maintain our client list. The problem is that many of us have spent most of our time throughout the years working for someone else, possibly far from the reach of our employer's customers. So, our customer service skills may be rusty, or even non-existent.

DOES IT REALLY MATTER?

Meager people skills and miniscule patience make some of us a business hazard when interacting with clients. Some people may not believe that this could be explosive to a freelancer's reputation, but according to a 2009 online survey by Tealeaf, there is cause for concern:

> *The survey results also show that online adults are increasingly turning to social media to share their online experiences with others, while simultaneously becoming less likely to alert a company directly — a shift in consumer behavior which extends the business impact of customer experience issues beyond any single transaction.*
>
> *http://www.marketwire.com/press-release/Tealeaf-Announces-Real-Time-Customer-Experience-Management-1169101.htm*

Given this trend among consumers, we can assume that the same would hold true for our freelance clients, and that the impact of the customer's experience will be felt long after the experience concludes. This makes it ever more critical for us to maintain as much control as possible over what that impact is, negative or positive.

This is important for freelancers adrift in the design and development ocean, where even the biggest among us still look small compared to the agency sharks that we compete with for work. If a client leaves with a bad taste in her mouth and decides to portray our business in an unflattering light, we have fewer resources than those sharks to seek out and address these word-of-mouth reviews in social media. Bigger businesses have more time, tools, and employees to scour social media outlets for mentions of their companies and to rectify complaints.

This was demonstrated to me recently when we awoke to find our Internet access down. After the standard panic and resetting of system, router, and modem, we determined that the problem did not stem from our end but rather from our provider's. Suddenly, we realized that, without a phone book in the building or access to the Internet or to our invoices (which we receive by email, doing what we can to be as paperless as possible), we did not have the phone number of our provider anywhere in the house. After a frustrating hour, we were finally back online and a bit steamed from our time off from being connected. Did we then contact the provider to vent or inquire about the problem? No. We did what Tealeaf's survey predicted we'd do: we turned to Twitter.

Having mentioned the company by name on Twitter, we were easy to find. Almost immediately, our provider read what we had to say and responded to us on this social media outlet, making sure we were not experiencing any more problems with connectivity. Overall, it made for an interesting lesson in customer service, and it showed where we as small fish might be missing opportunities to nip bad word of mouth in the bud before it spreads into viral gospel. As freelancers who wear every hat in the business ourselves, our time is limited, so we cannot stay on top of every mention of our business out there.

The number of consumers who contact a company directly in response to online transaction issues declined:
26% of online adults who experience problems conducting online transactions then posted complaints on a company's Website in 2009, versus 32% in 2008.
38% of all online adults contacted a company's call center after encountering problems using the Website in 2009, versus 47% in 2008.

http://www.tealeaf.com/news/news-releases/2010/Tealeaf-Announces-Real-Time-Customer-Experience-Management.php

The survey also reports that more than half of adults who spend time online have been influenced by social media in their consumer choices, which reinforces the importance of customer service to the health and growth of our freelancing businesses. A first impression no longer carries as much weight as it once did; each interaction with our clients bears as much on our business as another. We may think that as long as our business dealings end on a high note, that the rocky road that led there will not play a factor in the success of our freelancing career. A 2007 study released by Harris Interactive says different, suggesting that each dealing with our clients needs to be handled with care:

> The study reported that 80% of 2,049 US adults surveyed decided never to go back to a business/organization after a bad customer service experience. The study clearly indicates that an organization's customer service level is a defining factor that will make or break a company... Consumers have increasingly higher expectations of businesses and are willing to walk away quickly from a majority of businesses if those expectations are not met.
>
> *http://www.cmocouncil.org/programs/current/customer_voice/resources/*
> *Customer-Experience-Impact-Report.pdf*

The data shows that each and every interaction we have with a client is an opportunity to improve our business standing, because consumers are quicker to go elsewhere after a negative interaction. Even if our strengths do not lie in customer service, we need to ensure that each experience, whenever it occurs during the course of a project, is an agreeable one. Again, as freelancers, we have to deal with our clients at every stage of the project, and so we have to address not only the requirements of the project, but also any customer service issues that may arise in the process.

WHAT CAN WE DO?

We can do several things to improve our chances of getting positive results from all of our customer interactions. Of course, no one is guaranteed to satisfy all of their clients' needs and expectations 100% of the time, but we can take steps in the right direction. It starts with taking as much responsibility as we can for the impressions we leave with our customers.

BE FRIENDLY

This one almost goes without saying, but it should be considered from another perspective. Given that the majority of our interactions with our clients might be online, we need to remember that tone and intent does not always translate well to this medium.

So, read through your communications to catch anything that may come off negatively. We always want to be aware of the impression we're making in these seemingly minor moments. As shown before, the weight of an experience is felt long after the moment has passed.

BE PATIENT

Remember that your client probably does not share your level of expertise in your field. Their questions may not be clear and their feedback not as constructive as it needs to be. Put yourself in their position and be as patient as you would want someone else to be with you. Even if patience is not your strong suit, your customers want to feel that you are listening to and considering their opinions. If you switch off because they cannot communicate with you in your mode of parlance or you dismiss their feedback because they don't know as much as you do, you will be hurting your business more than your client.

BE ACCESSIBLE

Another thing that frustrates clients is lacking access to you when they need it most. As freelancers, we pride ourselves on our flexibility and being able to set our own hours. But we have to respect the hours during which our clients work, too, and make ourselves available at those times, so that they are able to share ideas and discuss progress in a back-and-forth conversation. One-sided conversations can easily be misinterpreted without further explanation and just delay the client from achieving his goal.

BE INFORMATIVE

One of the things Aaron Irizarry said in a recent videocast (www.this isaaronslife.com/friday-vidcast-10-30-09/) stuck out. He advised us to mind the skill gap between us and clients and to bridge these informational gaps whenever possible. Help them understand our processes and the reasons for the decisions we make. This gives them more faith in following our advice and increases the chances that they will return as clients.

KEEP TRACK AND GET BACK

When I mentioned that larger firms have more resources to invest in the customer service outlets that are available to all of us, I didn't mean that we shouldn't use those outlets at all. Take advantage of them to track what is said about your skills, or lack thereof, and respond accordingly. You may not be able to respond immediately, but do it when you can. If you find a criticism, consider the points they raise and address them thoughtfully, not dismissively. If they praise you, be gracious and return the gesture in kind.

BE PROACTIVE WITH MISTAKES

As I said in "Critical Mistakes Freelancers Make," we are all human, and mistakes happen. Don't shy away from them or, worse, neglect to acknowledge them at all. Own up to them. This is a time to shine by proactively addressing mistakes before they become an issue that the client feels compelled to bring to your (and other people's) attention.

You'll show your commitment to the client and project, and it will speak volumes about your character. By owning up to our mistakes, we show pride in our work, and more often than not the client will understand and forgive us.

GO ABOVE AND BEYOND

Doing all of the above usually puts you in the "above and beyond" category, but you could always push your freelancing business over the top by over-delivering. By giving your client more than they have asked for, you further demonstrate your commitment to making them happy and your pride in your performance. This can be as simple as addressing customer service concerns positively and proactively. It also encourages your clients to come back to you time and again.

Robert Bowen is an emerging author, celebrated podcaster, and poet. He is the co-founder and imaginative co-contributor of the creative design and blogging duo at the Arbenting Blog and Dead Wings Designs.

6

CREATIVELY HANDLING THE ADMIN SIDE OF FREELANCING

by Robert Bowen

THERE ARE VERY few who would argue against the notion that most freelance professionals, especially those operating in the design/development and writing arenas, tend to operate from a creative base. They are, by and large, a group that has chosen to let the right side of their brain steer them as far as the road stretches out before them. They embrace their creative and artistic nature, merging it into their career path and never looking back. And for the most part, a creative mind fits well in this freelance environment because they ultimately call all the shots and are bound by very few restraints — for the most part.

This road, however, is not without its bumps, and for a lot of freelancers, these bumps come when the left brain must be engaged to navigate the terrain.

Most of us are familiar with the concept of right brain versus left brain, wherein it has been shown that the two hemispheres of the brain control different modes of thinking. The right is the creative and artistic side, while the left is more logical and analytical.

Given that most of us are less apt to be full-minded (meaning we excel in both modes of thinking), there tend to be some issues when it comes time for you to mentally cross over for a short time to the other side. This can be a problem in freelancing, because though we might prefer to turn right, we have to handle every aspect of our business and that means every so often going left.

The administrative side of the job tends to be left-brain-heavy, and can prove difficult for some right-brainers to tackle. Below, I have broken down the offending areas that often hang us up, and have provided some tips for how to make it through these left-brained business barriers.

SCHEDULING

The first administrative task we will look at is scheduling, not only because of its importance to our freelance business, but because effective time management can aid with the other elements of your admin responsibilities. This tends to be very difficult for extremely creative individuals for the simple fact that right-brainers tend to be more random and less sequential in thought. And since scheduling creativity is not something we can always effectively manage, we tend to overlook the idea of scheduling our work altogether.

Ironically, this admin element, often avoided by creative types, can actually help stimulate our creative workflow. Scheduling different left-brained administrative tasks to be handled throughout the day offers your creative mind a change of gears. It essentially unplugs you from the mindset you're in when you create and gives your often overworked right brain a bit of a break. So when you return to the right side of things, you do so refreshed and recharged. Scheduling your day, therefore, can benefit both sides of your freelance business.

TIPS FOR TACKLING SCHEDULING

- The more fun that a tool is for you to use, the more likely it is that you're going to use it. Find an easy-to-use time management app with a fun UI and you will find that it is easier to motivate yourself to open it up and dive in.

- Be strict with yourself about all the self-imposed schedules you have come up with. By enforcing the schedules and through repetition, they will eventually become second nature and will be easier to work into your routine.

- Do not be too hard on yourself; just let your system evolve with you. Chances are, you are going to have a period of adjustment for this, so let it evolve and grow to suit you better rather than get frustrated and give up. The better the fit, the better it will serve your business.

- Always set yourself up with a redundancy system! Given that you may not be used to scheduling yourself, it may behoove you to have a backup plan. Having the extra coverage may also provide some peace of mind.

ACCOUNTING

The next administrative task we'll talk about is the bookkeeping side of business. I have always had an aversion to numbers, math, and anything accounting related, so this was a big adjustment for me as I imagine it has been for a lot of other freelancers. The easy answer for these woes is to simply hire an accountant, but for some — especially those just starting out in the business — this is not necessarily an affordable plan of attack. So we have to take these tasks upon ourselves and be able to make sense of it all.

The great thing about this area of your freelance life is that so many application authors understand our pain and they have developed wonderful programs that take most of the guesswork out of the equation. Client, account, and project management are becoming easier-than-ever for the right-brained inhabitants with applications. In these cases the software essentially handles most of this for you, while you simply input a bit of data.

TIPS FOR TACKLING ACCOUNTING

- Find a program that is suited to your needs only. The bells and whistles that go above and beyond are not necessary, and may only cause confusion. Especially in the beginning, keep it simple so you do not get overwhelmed.

- Make sure that you stay on top of these tasks. The bookkeeping is what keeps you going and stable, so make sure you do not get behind in your billing . . . that's the client's job. Set billing reminders and collection reminders so that you do not let anything fall through the cracks.

- The less time a task takes to get done, the less apt we are to put it off. Creating templates for your accounting paperwork can help cut down the time and thought that has to go into it. And that will naturally make you more prone to tackling the task.

- Help avoid penalties for your accounting practices. Each country and province has different laws and regulations that govern a business and the taxes that accompany it. Be sure that you find out what they are and keep up with changes to avoid accumulating penalties and fines.

CORRESPONDENCE

Another aspect of the administrative side to your freelance business that will often draw periods of procrastination is your business correspondence. This is not referring to replying to a pen pal or any kind of creative writing; this generally is detailed and contractual writing, which immediately presents itself as a barrier to the right-brained thinkers. So it is a natural reaction for the creatively minded to avoid dealing with the inbox or returning messages that we cannot deny are important. Even though this is not occurring face-to-face, we still feel out of our element, so we put off until tomorrow what should have been done today.

Once again, the right-brainers tend to think more randomly than sequentially, so communicating our thoughts to those populating the opposite sphere can prove problematic. But this is where the scheduling can further assist you. Most of our business runs on some form of back-and-forth communication — be it with clients, users, colleagues, etc. — so making time every day to sort through your inbox will keep it running smoothly. Getting back in a timely fashion will reflect positively on you and build trust in your brand.

TIPS FOR TACKLING CORRESPONDENCE

- Again, get time on your side and this will help get you going. If you find that you are regularly responding to the same types of queries, create copy templates to move your mail along.
- Prioritize and categorize and the task will fly past. Keeping a hierarchy of your correspondence and keeping it separated by types will keep you rolling through quick and easy. Again, this breaking down and separating of your messages may not be the easiest for the right-brainers to build into a habit, but it is certainly worth a try.
- Get in and get out! Try to keep your inbox empty and your messages filed away for easy reference and prioritization. If it is a message that can be replied to quickly, then go ahead and immediately get this done; otherwise file it for later.
- Brevity is beyond key; it is your best friend. Keep your correspondence brief and to the point and avoid venturing down unnecessary avenues that leave you open to further questions. If you ramble on, you are simply wasting time that you could be using elsewhere.

CLIENT RELATIONS

Another oftentimes administrative nightmare that freelancers come across is the client relations portion of the position. There is a reason we like the solitude that tends to accompany the freelance career path, and so breaking out of that solitary shell to be able to effectively communicate with clients can be daunting. It's no secret that in order for your business to thrive, you need to have a client base to build upon. And as should be no secret to anyone, the way you deal with your clients will often determine if they will return.

As a creative individual whose train of thought pulls right, interacting with those on the left side of the tracks will not always go smoothly. In fact, it may not translate well. The means and methods that right-brainers subscribe to, even in explanations and conversations, can tend to be hard to follow for lefters, and vice versa. So it is imperative that we try to make an effort to keep these interactions focused and on topic. And by understanding that such a translation gap exists, we can make more of an effort to bridge the gap when we deal with our clients.

TIPS FOR TACKLING CLIENT RELATIONS

- Try to step outside your regular right-brained random ways. Momentarily leave them behind and organize your thoughts before meetings. Taking notes and outlining the points you need to cover beforehand can help you stay focused and have an easier time following along.
- Just as you are often responsible for steering clients toward a decision once they employ you, you need to continue to make strides toward being able to steer the conversation. This helps to ensure you stay comfortable as you converse, and it keeps you in your element as much as possible.
- Since it is necessary to understand the project from every angle, have your clients explain their approach from many directions. This may help you find a way to relate to it when you otherwise wouldn't.
- It may sound cheesy, but you may want to set up dry-run practices with some of your non-creative friends or family. Running through your side of the conversation with someone who does not work from a creative place may prepare you for meetings with clients.

BACKUPS AND UPDATES

When it comes to important administrative tasks that so many freelancers tend to let slip through the cracks, keeping up with backups and updates ranks high on the list for right-brainers. Creative people tend to work in the moment of inspiration, and we are enveloped by that moment. But the moment moves on, and when it does move on, we are swallowed up by the next task. With our ever-forward-moving momentum pushing against us, we forget to look back, let alone back up (. . . sorry). And stopping in the middle of our creative flow to update our software doesn't exactly rank high either.

Naturally, as a freelancer you are going to be the only one managing and keeping records of what is happening on your end, including those ever-precious works-in-progress. Losing them would be devastating, but remembering to back them up wouldn't exactly be a right-brainer move . . . though I think it may be a both-brain sphere issue. It seems that most of us do not consider backing up our files until something actually happens to cause a drive to crash and we lose them all. But again, in the freelance field you are on your own when it comes to data loss; there is no IT department backing you up, so to speak.

TIPS FOR TACKLING UPDATES AND BACKUPS

- Automation is a right-brainer's buddy, and it just means that you may actually get your backups and updates done! Finding a service that backs up your data automatically takes the stress off you and ensures that you won't have to worry about any right-brained interference in this area.

- Take a moment, and take a hike! For many of us, as long as we are at our computer, we will not have the willpower to stop working and get our backups and updates done. So walk away. Give yourself a break, start the process and come back later ready to go.

- A lot of basic software updates are quick and easy and do not interrupt your workflow for very long. Scheduling can definitely work with you in this arena, as most productivity methods encourage you to take short breaks throughout your work day. Set up to run updates during these breaks so that you know they get done.

- Once again, turn to prioritization and a left-brained-style breakdown to get over the procrastination hump that bars most creative types (and so many more) from getting their updates and backups done. Decide what are your most important files and programs, and make sure that they get done first and foremost. Then as you work through your week, work through your lower-priority items.

GENERAL ADVICE

Now for some more generic suggestions for creative types.

YOU ARE CREATIVE, SO ACT LIKE IT!

Overall, you cannot ignore your administrative responsibilities and hope they go away. So do what it is that you do best — approach these tasks creatively. The interwebs are alive with creative solutions to so many different problems that you are bound to be able to find one that fits yours. If not, maybe come up with your own. Nothing is out of reach for the creative mind, because we know no limitations… even the occasional cross-over to the left side.

INSPIRATION IS THE EASY PART, NOW LET'S TALK MOTIVATION!

One of the hardest things for most creative-minded individuals to do when approaching the territory of the left is getting motivated to tackle these tasks. Even those of us not prone to procrastination will tend to let the left-side work pile up longer than the right simply because it is a less comfortable fit for us. The thing to remember is that getting started is usually the hardest part. Force yourself to get started, and let it roll. Immerse yourself in as much of a creative environment as you can to help smooth the transition, and run with it!

DO NOT ELABORATE, THAT JUST COMPLICATES!

You know if it rhymes it's got to be true (even though that absolute doesn't rhyme, but still . . .). Another important thing to remember is to keep things simple to help with these momentary forays into foreign territories. Remember that this is not where your strengths lie, so it may be best for you not to take on too much in one bite. Keep things as concise and brief as you can, taking them a piece at a time. As right-brained thinkers we tend to see things as a whole rather than in parts, so try to find the different parts and break them down, tackling one at a time. That was the reason for breaking everything apart above, so that you could see a way to start separating the different parts from the whole. This can make the tasks at hand seem less overwhelming.

IT'S IN YOUR REACH, YOU JUST HAVE TO GO FOR IT!

An important thing to remember, overall, is that just because we tend to prefer one mode of thinking (be it right- or left-brained), we can improve our abilities within each side through exercises that stimulate the different hemispheres. The problem tends to arise when there is an imbalance in educational focus that fails to appeal to both sides of the brain. This doesn't mean it is beyond us, just that we have not worked at improving the opposite sphere. So the more that we keep those sides stimulated, the easier the tasks that fall to that side of the brain will be to take on.

Robert Bowen is an emerging author, celebrated podcaster, and poet. He is the co-founder and imaginative co-contributor of the creative design and blogging duo at the Arbenting Blog and Dead Wings Designs.

7 PITCHING LIKE A PRO

by Cameron Chapman

CORRESPONDENCE WITH POTENTIAL clients is vital to securing new work. Being able to write a competent, persuasive proposal as well as a professional cover letter and other letters (or emails) can set a designer apart from his or her less professional competition.

The idea of crafting a formal proposal can be intimidating to many designers. But a good proposal can land you clients and set the tone for your relationship with those clients. It's worth the time and effort to learn to create a compelling proposal that will convince prospective clients that you're the designer for them.

48

What follows is a guide to creating a professional proposal, broken down by section, as well as some tips for writing great cover letters to accompany your proposals. There are also hints at convincing prospects to sign with you instead of your competition at the end.

ANATOMY OF A PROFESSIONAL PROPOSAL

The web design proposal is one of the most important documents in the client-designer relationship. It serves multiple functions: an outline of the project, a contract between the client and designer, and a method for clarifying what the project is all about.

Exactly how you format your proposal is up to you, but there are certain parts that virtually every proposal should include. Feel free to get creative in the design of the proposal, but remember that the primary purpose is to convey information. Anything that interferes with the readability of the document should be cut.

COVER PAGE

Every proposal should have a cover page. This cover page needs to contain some basic information about what the document contains. Mainly, it should include the following points:

- A line that says something like: "Website Design Proposal for XYZ Company."
- Who prepared the proposal, including company name and contact information.
- You might also wish to include your company's nondisclosure statement here.

The cover page makes it easy for your client to immediately identify what the document is and who it's from. Anything you can do to make it easier for your prospective client to get in touch with you (or just remember who you are), is a positive thing for you.

NONDISCLOSURE STATEMENT

A nondisclosure statement should always be present on any proposal you send to a client, no matter how informal that proposal is. Many clients don't realize there's anything wrong with taking the ideas of one designer and sharing them with another designer. Many also don't realize that sharing information about how you format your proposals, what you include, and what your rates are, is often sensitive internal information that should not be shared with your competitors.

While a nondisclosure statement will do little to deter shady clients from sharing your proposal's content with another design firm, it can do a lot to deter clients who just don't know any better. In any event, including one is an important legal protection. Whether you want to have a formal, legal nondisclosure statement drafted by a lawyer or simply state something in plain language is up to you. But the statement should basically say that all the information contained in the proposal is the property of your design firm and should not be shared with anyone without prior written authorization.

COMPANY STATEMENT

Your company statement is a surprisingly important part of any design proposal. This is where you get to give the client a little information that will set your company apart from competing firms. Stress your strengths here, as well as any pertinent information that makes you particularly qualified for their project.

Your company statement should include a little background on your company, as well as your company philosophy or mission statement. But keep the whole thing short; a couple of paragraphs is ideal, but no more than a page under any circumstances. If you go longer, you risk your client skimming that part of the proposal in favor of getting to the details of their project.

CLIENT INFORMATION

The client information should state not only the name of the company and their contact information, but also your particular contact at the company. There should also be a brief, one-line description of the project here.

CLIENT GOALS

This section should outline what the client's project aims to do. Consider whether the site they're seeking bids for will be an e-commerce site, a social network, or something else. You should have sought this information prior to writing the proposal, and should have a good idea of what the client is looking for. If not, you'll need to ask the client some questions about what they're looking for.

If there are specific objectives already outlined for the project, a bulleted list can work really well for this section. Otherwise, just a paragraph or two that describes the project as you understand it is sufficient.

SPECIAL CONSIDERATIONS

This is a pretty broad area, but almost every project will have at least a few special considerations. You need to outline them right in the proposal, and consider their impacts on your overall timeline and costs. What, exactly, these specific considerations are is likely to vary substantially between different projects and different clients. A few examples:

- A site aimed at children will need to follow certain legal guidelines regarding content and parental permissions.
- A site for disabled users will need to have special attention paid to accessibility issues.

- The design might need to smoothly transition from an older design, following a similar layout or color scheme.
- There could be special bandwidth or storage needs if the site will be hosting a lot of multimedia files or will be particularly high-traffic.

Of course, there are potentially hundreds of different "special considerations" you may need to account for in the design process. Outlining as many as you can in the proposal stage will help to ensure there are fewer misunderstandings later in the process.

It also helps to reassure your client that you're really listening to their needs and will come up with a comprehensive solution that works for their company.

PROPOSED SOLUTION

This section should offer a brief description of how you propose to meet the goals of the client. General terms like "e-commerce site" or "social network" are key here, as this section will be followed by more specifics.

Keep this section to less than a page, preferably a couple of paragraphs that outline what types of content will be included on the site, as well as the general functionality the site will possess. Again, you'll get into more specifics in subsequent sections.

PROJECT SPECIFICS

This is the real meat of the proposal. This is where you outline specifically what the site will consist of. An itemized list of exactly what work you're proposing to do should be included.

The list should include a brief description of any part that isn't obvious. Keep these descriptions to a couple of sentences at most, or break them down into smaller parts. This section should give your client an idea of exactly what they're getting for their money.

Depending on the type of site you're designing, you might include here specific plugins that will be used (or created), as well as any custom artwork you'll be creating for the client. It's not uncommon for this section to run well over a page, and oftentimes much longer for complicated or particularly large sites.

PROJECT PHASES

This is where you want to outline exactly how long each part of the project will take. For example, you might propose taking two weeks to provide wireframes or an initial mockup. You might then give the client one week to approve those or suggest changes.

Make sure you outline both your parts and theirs. Emphasize that it's important they meet the deadlines you've set if they want to keep the project on schedule. It's also a good idea to overestimate how much time things will take you, as it's better to under-promise and over-deliver than the other way around. It can also be helpful to sometimes give your clients tighter deadlines, as it creates a sense of urgency and often motivates them to take care of things immediately rather than waiting until the last minute.

Using specific dates rather than just a general timeline can also add a sense of urgency. If you opt not to set specific dates in the proposal, specify that you'll provide them with a finalized schedule once the contract has been signed.

Some designers may opt to include the project phases within the section on project specifics. This can work well for relatively simple projects, but for complex projects it may be confusing. It's best to decide this on a case-by-case basis.

MAINTENANCE PLAN

It's a good idea to include information on a monthly maintenance plan for your clients in the proposal. Outline what your regular maintenance agreement consists of and how many hours of work that includes. Also specify whether any unused time can be rolled over into subsequent months.

Include here whether hosting is included in the monthly maintenance plan or if that's a separate cost. Also include here information on your timelines for maintenance or updates. Clients want to know up front whether your typical turnaround time is a day or a week.

FEES

You'll need to outline exactly what your fees are for the project. Itemizing to some extent is often helpful for clients. Also specify whether this estimate may change, and under what circumstances. Letting clients know that delays on their part or extra rounds of revisions will add to the cost is something that's often overlooked by designers. And if it's not pointed out to clients in the proposal stage, they may dispute extra charges later.

Giving clients information about how the project is being charged can sometimes be helpful in landing the project, but can also be detrimental. Many clients don't care how many hours something will take you; they're only interested in the final costs. Of course, other clients want to know exactly what they're paying for, and will request a more detailed breakdown of charges. This is another thing you'll need to tailor to the particular client.

Another thing to include here is the payment schedule, including how much of a deposit is required before you start work. Unless you've worked successfully with the client before, you should always get a deposit before you begin work. Some designers charge a small amount, only 10% or so, while others might require as much as half of the total up front. This is also largely dependent on the scope of the project, the overall timeline, and the total charges.

NEXT STEPS

Detailing exactly what the client needs to do to get the ball rolling on their project is something that's often overlooked. Using the proposal as a contract can often work better than having a separate document that basically lays out exactly the same thing. Including a line for them to sign as well as instructions for sending whatever deposit you require to get started can prompt a client to sign with you.

Including a deadline for the client to sign the proposal and get it back to you can also increase your chances of getting a signed contract. Telling them that if they get the signed contract back to you by X date for you to start work by Y date can be a strong motivator. After all, clients are often eager to get their project underway.

FORMATTING YOUR PROPOSAL

Your proposal should be formatted like any business correspondence. It should emphasize the content over all else. It should be easy to read and nothing should distract from what it says. Including a logo or similar graphics on the cover page is fine.

If you're going to email the proposal, converting it to a PDF before sending will help ensure that it's seen by your prospective client the way you intend it to be seen. Make sure you check your file size before emailing it, and try to make sure it's less than 1MB to prevent any transmission problems. Always attach your proposal; never include it in the body of the email.

If you're going to mail it, make sure you use a good quality paper, but don't go overboard. A high quality, bright white printer paper is fine. There's no need to use something fancy like a cotton paper or résumé paper. Make sure your printer toner or ink isn't running out and is printing sufficiently dark. Review the final document in its printed form before mailing it to make sure there were no printing problems.

COVER LETTERS AND BUSINESS CORRESPONDENCE

Whenever you're sending a document for a client to review, you should include a cover letter. It makes the entire package look more professional, and makes sure your client knows exactly what it is they've just received. In the case of a proposal, it helps set the tone for a professional client-designer relationship.

STANDARD BUSINESS FORMAT

Your cover letter should follow established business-letter format. This means it should include the following parts, in order:

- The date, formatted as: "day month, year" or "month day, year"
- Your address, unless it's included somewhere on your letterhead
- The client name and address
- The salutation (Dear Mr. X, or similar)
- The body of the letter. Keep this professional, use proper capitalization and punctuation, and only make it as long as it needs to be.
- The closing (Sincerely, or something equally professional)
- Your signature
- Your name and title, typed
- If there are any enclosures
- If the letter has been CC'd to anyone

Cover letters should be printed on your letterhead, on good quality paper. Make sure you use a font that's professional and readable (a good rule of thumb is to use at least an 11 pt. font, and preferably a 12 pt. font). Your cover letter should rarely run more than a single page.

BUSINESS LETTERS

Cover letters aren't the only business letters you're likely to send in your career. For the most part, though, you'll be corresponding by email more than mail. It's tempting to be very casual in an email, but this is a very bad idea when dealing with prospects and clients, especially new ones.

Whenever you're corresponding with a client or prospect, always use proper grammar and punctuation, capitalization, and other standards you would use in a printed business letter. Avoid using emoticons or slang, at least until after the client has done so. Even then, they should be used sparingly.

Just because something is being transmitted electronically isn't an excuse to be less professional than you would be in a mailed letter. Always remember that you're engaging in business correspondence and act accordingly. Create a professional signature to include in every email you send that includes your name and title, phone number, preferred email address, and website address, as well as other pertinent contact information.

SPECIAL EMAIL CONSIDERATIONS

If you're emailing your proposal, you'll want to write the cover letter in the body of the email. There are some formatting considerations you'll want to take into account when emailing your cover letter rather than printing it out. First of all, omit everything above the salutation in standard business letter format. Start with "Dear Mr. X," or similar.

At the end of your email, below your signature, you'll want to include your contact information, rather than at the top of the email. You can omit the "CC'd" section at the end, as it will be apparent in the header of the email if it's been CC'd. You can also generally omit the "enclosures" section, as it should be apparent what's been attached to the email. You may want to mention any attachments in the body of the email, though, so that your recipient knows what they're opening.

CONVINCING CLIENTS

Even with an excellent written proposal and cover letter, you may have times when a client is hesitant to sign with you or your company. A lot of designers at this point will simply wait for the company to make up their mind. They're so afraid of coming across as pushy or like they're going for the "hard sell" that they don't go for any sale at all.

There are ways you can persuade a prospect to sign with you, though, that aren't pushy and won't make you come across like a used car salesman.

STRESS YOUR STRENGTHS

When you're trying to convince a prospective client to hire you, you need to stress why you're the perfect person or team for their project. Think about the things they need and how you can provide those things. Keep reiterating to them that you have the skills they need.

Provide evidence of those skills. Show them other projects you've taken on and how what you did in those instances can be applied to their project. Proof of your strengths and competencies can be a powerful persuasive tool.

DON'T DISPARAGE COMPETITORS

When a client tells you they're trying to decide between you and a competing design firm, it can be tempting to point out all the flaws in that other firm. The temptation grows even stronger when there are real, identifiable problems that the other firm is trying to hide. Resist that temptation!

In a best case scenario, you disparaging your competition is likely to have little effect on the client's decision. In a worst case scenario, it looks like you've got sour grapes over something or other, and actually works in your competitor's favor. If there are real problems with the competitor (a history of unethical practices or unfinished projects, for example), simply urge your prospective client to check references for both you and the competitor before making their decision.

ASK QUESTIONS, OFFER SOLUTIONS

If a client is on the fence, ask them questions about why they're having a hard time deciding. Then address their answers directly. Find solutions to their concerns. In many cases, they might just be confused about some part of the process or your proposal (or your competitor's proposal).

Open and honest communication with prospective clients will lead to better client-designer relationships in the long run. You'll have a clearer understanding of exactly what they want, and they'll feel comfortable asking you questions about the process or otherwise communicating when they're confused about something. This generally results in happier clients in the end and less stressed designers during the project itself.

THINGS TO WATCH OUT FOR

If a client seems impossible to satisfy, you may be better off walking away from the project. If they're unable to make a decision during the proposal stage, it's only likely to get worse as the project progresses. You want to work with clients who can make decisions and meet deadlines. Clients who can't do either only result in headaches for the designer and are rarely completely happy with the finished result.

Another thing to watch out for is a client who's constantly trying to get you to come down on price or to throw in extras without charging for them. While sometimes this is just indicative of a budget-conscious client, it can also mean that the client is going to try to nickel-and-dime you on every part of the project, will dispute charges, and possibly even delay or neglect to pay their bills.

OVERCOMING SPECIFIC CONCERNS

Sometimes when a client can't make up their mind, it seems completely arbitrary. They don't give you enough information about why they're hesitant to hire you to effectively convince them with anything but generalities. But in other cases, they give you specific reasons why they're unsure about hiring you. When this happens, it's an opportunity. They're giving you the chance to overcome their objections, as well as all the information you need to do so.

There are a number of common concerns clients have. And each one can be overcome once you know what their hesitation is based on. Here are some of the most common concerns clients have, and what you can do in response.

SCOPE AND SCALE OF THE PROJECT

After reviewing your carefully crafted proposal, some clients may get cold feet and say they only want to tackle part of the project at that time. In most cases this is related to either the time involved in the project or the price. You'll need to find out which one it is, and the easiest way to do so is to ask. Be upfront and simply ask them if it's the timeline for the project or the budget that makes them want to only complete part of the project at this time.

If it's the timeline for the project, suggest sticking to the proposed schedule (or a slightly modified one), but rolling out new features as they're completed, rather than waiting for the entire site to be finished before launching the new site. Adjust the schedule if necessary to make sure each part of the project is modularized so parts of the site can be rolled out separately. Then, adjust the payment schedule so payment is made for each section launched. This helps assure you won't end up completing more work than you're paid for if the project stalls or is put on hold by the client.

If it's price the client is concerned with, you'll likely need to come up with a plan to stretch the project over a longer time period. You can also propose a compromise, with a bit more than what they're proposing for the project, but short of the entire proposal. If the client has decided they don't want to spend as much money as they'd originally planned, there's often not much you can do to overcome that. Instead, work with the client within the new budget. The goal here is to make them very happy with the first phase of the project so they'll then be eager to move on with the rest. There's more on overcoming price objections later in this section.

EFFECTIVENESS

Clients often have high hopes for their website when they first start out. They hope it will bring them more customers and more money. But as they move along in the process, they often start to doubt those original goals. This is often due to honest feedback and guidance from designers, who don't want them to have unrealistic expectations from their site. But it can quickly spiral out of control and suddenly those once-enthusiastic clients are wondering if there's even any point in a new website.

At this point, it's usually a good idea to give the client a pep talk. Ask them again what they're hoping to get out of the website, and then give them concrete information on how your proposal will help them meet those goals. Remind them that a new website isn't going to miraculously improve their business, but it's an important facet of a successful marketing and sales plan for many businesses. Don't over-promise, but be positive and remind them why they wanted a new website in the first place.

EXPERIENCE

This can be a tough one to overcome. Let's say your prospective client has proposals from a number of designers they're considering, and you're the least experienced. While sometimes coming in at a lower price than your more experienced competitors can be enough to entice the client to take a chance, in other cases they're more concerned with results than money.

The thing to do here is to reassure them that you have the necessary skills to get their project done. Point them to previous successful projects you've completed, and give them testimonials or references to back up your claims. Tell them that your price reflects the fact that you have less experience, but that you're confident you can complete their project successfully. In many cases, if you're confident you can do the work, it will transfer to the client, and they'll gain confidence that you know what you're doing.

ACCESSIBILITY TO YOU

This can be a big concern to many clients. They want to know that if they have a question or need to get in touch with you, that you'll be accessible to them. People are used to 24-hour support lines and instant answers when they run into a problem. But in most cases, designers can't be quite that accessible.

Remind your client of all the different ways they can get in touch with you, and let them know that you'll be available should an emergency with their website arise. Let them know what your policy is when you go on vacation or are sick (is there someone else who handles things while you're gone or do you handle emergency work personally, even if you're sitting on the beach in Cabo?) and assure them that you won't drop off the face of the earth at the exact time they're website crashes due to a huge increase in sales.

TIME REQUIRED ON THEIR PART AND YOURS

If your client plans to keep their website updated themselves, they may be concerned about how much time that will require. Some clients may envision having to hire an entire new staff member just to keep their website updated. The best way to overcome this is to give them a sneak peek into the CMS their site will be built on. Show them how easy it will be for them to add a new image or change around some text. If you're using a good CMS, this should set their mind at ease.

If the client wants you to be able to do updates to their site, you may need to reassure them that a) you have time to keep their site updated and won't take weeks to make simple changes, and b) that it won't take you hours and hours every month to make simple changes that will end up costing them hundreds or thousands of dollars. Giving them an estimate of how much time different basic updates take, as well as reminding them of your policy on minimum charges, will make them less wary of huge unexpected maintenance charges in the future.

CONTENT OWNERSHIP

This concern is sometimes surprising for many designers. Clients often wonder who actually owns their website, both the content on it and the site itself. This can be exacerbated if you're also offering them hosting and domain registration services. They want to know what happens if they decide to move their site to a different host or if they want to make changes in the future with a different designer.

Make sure there's something in your proposal or contract that states that as long as their bills with you are current, their website and all content on it are their property. Let them know that at any point they can switch web hosts or designers and you'll help facilitate that change (at your normal hourly rate) in whatever way is necessary. Assure your clients that the content they put up on their site is their property, and that the site itself is also theirs.

You may want to put a clause in this, though, that states that the code is your copyrighted material and is only offered to the client on a non-exclusive license. Otherwise, it's feasible that a client could sue you if they saw you designed a competitor's site and used similar or identical features. But assure them that this only applies to the code, not to the design or content.

PRICE

Sometimes the client's resistance is related to price. There are a ton of low-priced (and often low-quality) designers out there, undercutting the competition and enticing clients with big promises. It can be tempting, especially as a new designer, to try to match these competitors on price. But that's a bad idea for a few reasons: it undervalues your work, it makes clients come to expect low prices (which leads to even lower prices), and it sets a bad precedent for future work from that client. While sometimes offering a small discount to secure an account or to keep a long-term client happy is acceptable, it's a bad habit to get into.

Rather than trying to compete on price, compete on value. In all likelihood, if a company is undercutting your price by a lot, they're cutting corners in one way or another. Ask the client questions about what your competitor is offering. Then compare it to what you're promising them. Asking questions in a non-threatening manner can lead to the client more carefully scrutinizing what the competitor is actually telling them. Reassure the client that you stand behind your work, and while you can't guarantee results, you will guarantee that the website will be fully functional and supported.

If the competition is promising the moon for very little money, it can be a good idea to remind your prospect to get and check references, and to visit and use some of the sites within that company's portfolio. It also pays to remind them to be sure the competitor did the entire website, not just the design or coding. There are horror stories out there of people paying thousands for what they think will be a fully functioning website and in the end all they end up with are some PSD files and a company that won't answer their emails.

As mentioned before, you don't want to trash your competition. But that doesn't mean you can't encourage your prospective clients to carry out proper due diligence in choosing which firm to hire. Make sure, too, that you don't alienate the client if they decide to go with a different firm. If the sole reason was price (and it was a significant difference), chances are they may be unhappy with the finished product. You want them to come back to you if they decide to redo their site.

If the price issue has less to do with a competitor undercutting you and more to do with general sticker shock, meet with the client to discuss their budget needs in better detail. Try to come up with a solution that works for their budget. Again, be careful of prospects who are trying to nickel-and-dime you, but realize that sometimes people just don't realize how expensive a website can be. Consider working out phases of the project, so they don't have to pay everything all at once and can complete different phases as their budget allows. Working with a client and coming up with mutually beneficial solutions like this can be an excellent foundation to building a long-term relationship with a client who will not only bring you consistent work, but will also appreciate that you're sensitive to their business needs.

IN CONCLUSION

Creating a professional proposal is a key step in landing new clients. Spend the time and energy to create a custom proposal for each prospective client rather than using some boilerplate copy and you'll see your closing rates rise. A client who feels like you're paying specific attention to them, their needs, and their project will be more likely to hire you and will likely be happier with the end result.

Cameron Chapman is a professional web and graphic designer with over six years of experience. She writes for a number of blogs, including her own, Cameron Chapman On Writing. *She's also the author of* Internet Famous: A Practical Guide to Becoming an Online Celebrity.

8

THE FINANCES OF FREELANCING

by Luke Reimer

WE'RE NOT ACCOUNTANTS . . . We're web designers. Especially when working as an individual rather than as part of a team, many freelancers get caught up in focusing on the websites that they create rather than the necessary practices surrounding each project. These practices can aid in a number of ways, such as stress-relieving organization, more efficient time management, a better understanding of costs and pricing, and ultimately how your freelance work fits into your overall annual income.

THE FOUNDATION

Record keeping and analysis are foundational to financial efforts, whether we like it or not. Tracking time spent and corresponding tasks during a project is crucial to better understanding your freelance work from a high level. It doesn't need to entail an hour-by-hour log — even estimating time spent at the close of a project, when these figures are fresh in your mind, can do the trick. The bottom line is, before you can seek to improve or tighten up your freelance finances you need to accurately understand where you currently stand.

The three elements of keeping records are time, income, and expenses. If you can record these for each project, and how the three of these interact, you're in great shape to begin analyzing how you can better stay organized and even increase your revenues.

MAXIMIZING PROFIT

What steps can you take to maximize your profits? Here are a couple of suggestions.

■ *Provide a detailed invoice.* Our income as web designers is relatively straight forward — we get paid for a web project according to a price predetermined in project planning and client interaction. However, it's a good practice to develop a more detailed invoice than just the overall project cost. Common lines on your invoice can include administrative time spent documenting and organizing the project, overhead for managing contractors or project management, materials such as stock photography/fonts and any special software requirements, and conference calls, travel, and meetings. It can feel a little uncomfortable at first billing for things like administration or cost per kilometer for travel, but these are generally accepted practices that most clients engage in themselves.

■ *Follow best practices on quoting.* The project quote or bid is where your project income all begins. There are entire articles written on this topic alone — and it's best to do the research to determine both how to go about quoting a project with a client, and how to quote accurately (not too high, not too low).

It's important to engage in two specific practices when quoting: a needs analysis, and a market analysis. The needs analysis entails gathering every bit of relevant information pertaining to the project and what the client requires, and the market analysis involves assessing the current web market for the type of project, as well as your level of skill and experience (and that of your team members if applicable).

MINIMIZING EXPENSES

In addition to maximizing profit, you want to keep your expenses to a minimum.

■ *Use web tools.* There are literally hundreds of web apps, online tools, and open source downloads that can assist you in time management, invoicing, document templates, process mapping, and all sorts of tasks that occur throughout the design and development process as well as overall finances. Pick a few of these, but not all of them, and work them into your business model.

Pen and paper, or sporadic spreadsheets and documents, can only take you so far before they begin wasting your time rather than saving it. I find web tools particularly useful for time tracking, project management, invoicing, and streamlining communications.

■ *Streamline your process.* Be sure to develop a process to save time and prevent yourself from re-inventing the wheel with every project. There are some great web design process guides available — check them out! Other streamlining time-saving activities can involve drafting common emails, to-do lists, and leveraging collaboration tools.

AVOIDING PITFALLS

There are certainly some financial risks when it comes to freelancing that can leave you out in the cold. Some of these practices have helped keep me from getting burned, or have come about from experiencing some unfortunate situations in the past!

65

- *Fixed quotes from subcontractors.* This is something that I almost always demand, especially concerning a large project. Allowing sub-contractors to charge by the hour opens you up to serious risk, even if the individual in question is a trusted friend or associate. If he or she underestimates the tasks, unfortunately, that's their problem, not yours. After all, you're trying to run a business.

- *Clear financial communication.* It's essential to be open and clear about the finances of a project.

  - *With clients:* Being upfront about costs and expenses could very well be the number one rule to financial effectiveness in freelancing. Remaining clear about expenses at the beginning of a project is much easier than trying to justify them in the end. If all is laid out and the client understands what they will be charged and why they are being charged for it, they'll be happy to pay you. Surprises, on the other hand, can cause delays and conflicts.

  - *With subcontractors:* Clear financial communication is just as crucial when dealing with your team or your subcontractors. Make sure they are aware exactly what you will pay, when you will pay it, and conversely what you expect in return, and when you expect to get it.

- *Charge part of your project revenue up front.* It's common industry practice to charge a percentage of your project revenue up front — or at least a portion of it somewhere in the early stages. If you've practiced good client interaction, sales, and communication, the client shouldn't have a problem with this concept. This can also save your tail if the client for some reason decides to upset the project part-way through, and drives further commitment to contribute to the working relationship.

- *Back up your files.* It only takes one hard drive failure to burn this practice into your memory forever, and you'll never quite expect it when it comes. Prevent this type of scenario by backing up not only your web site files, but all of your records and financial data as well. It's a good policy even to make hard copies of certain important documents such as contracts and income statements.

The way I approach backing up information is the "fire mentality." If my flat or office burned to the ground, what would I have left? This means that beyond your computer, your external hard drives, and hard copies, you need to have additional or supplementary backup either online or at a separate location.

BANKING

While many of us start by working out of our kitchens or bedrooms as an individual freelancer, it's important to separate your personal finances from your business finances — especially if you're planning on expensing certain items to the business for tax deductions.

Start by meeting with someone from your local bank. They're generally happy to sit down by appointment and discuss your needs as a small business owner, and they can shed some great light on your financial situation stemming from their experience in the banking industry. Once you have a good handle on your options and what the standards are, open up a business bank account and start running your income and expenses through it rather than your personal account. That way everything is kept nicely separate and it's easy to view your business activity by checking out your account history.

If you expense equipment, travel, food, supplies, and the like to your business for tax deduction, be sure to keep a record of all receipts as hard copies as well as to enter the data electronically in some fashion (potentially using a web tool).

GOVERNMENT OR INSTITUTIONAL SUPPORT

It may be different depending on your geographic location, but it's always worth looking into. In Canada, for instance, there are a whole pile of resources aimed at helping small business owners succeed — these include small business centers in every major city for seminars, networking, and marketing, as well as applications for grants and loans from the government to help you on your way. It's worth looking into the support that may be available to you, whether it's simply a network or actual financial aid.

GETTING PERSONAL

And now for some advice on items closer to home.

GET A HIGH LEVEL PERSPECTIVE ON YOUR INCOME

Freelance income is often seriously sporadic, especially if it's a part time side gig as with most web designers. You do some work in what feels like your spare time, and you receive almost random influxes of cash as projects close or you move through payment schedules.

This style and type of income generation can be difficult to wrap your head around in comparison to a steady salary and a standard pay day once every few weeks that you'd receive from a full-time corporation. It's important to step back and understand how much you're actually earning, especially in comparison to the overall time you put into each project.

PERSONAL BUDGETING

Personal budgets are always a pain, unless you're the hyper-organized type. However, using the figures gleaned from financial estimates and calculations based on web projects can play a major role in organizing yourself economically.

Instead of "oh, and I'll probably make a couple grand here and there from web projects", it should ideally be, "last year my net income from web design was roughly $XXXXX, so I can factor this into my overall expenses and income."

TAXES

This is also a localized issue depending on what country you design out of, but it's a generally important piece of the puzzle to keep in mind throughout the entire year. All of your record keeping and tight organization will contribute to a much more stress-free tax filing season than a mad scramble to dig up receipts and old sent emails.

Be sure to investigate the protocols and limits for what you can expense to your business, as well as any other regulations. Web design income can be tempting to keep off of the books in certain situations, but in the long term it is rarely in your favor. You're much better off developing strong small business accounting practices and financial discipline to aid you in future work.

FINANCIAL PLANNING

Linking to the discussion of understanding your web design income from a high level, financial planning on a longer term scale is also important. When analyzing your personal income plan and having a birds-eye-view financial outlook, it's important to consider retirement planning as well as debt pay-down plans. Use the records you've begun to keep and your financial data from web income to assist these personal financial plans. The previously mentioned discussion with a banker can also be a good time to bring up these concepts.

CONCLUSION

It all comes down to spending the right time and effort to keep track, save the information, and then use it when necessary to accomplish tasks and administration at high efficiency. Estimation is a concept employed a great deal by web designers, and striving to make these estimations accurate should be a very high priority. With this information you can reach ideal revenue from projects, minimize your expenses with each new venture, and organize yourself financially for discipline and freedom from stress.

Luke Reimer is a web project manager, designer, and developer currently operating Fluid Media web design group out of Waterloo, Canada.

II

COMMUNICATION WITH CLIENTS AND PARTNERS

9

HOW TO IDENTIFY AND DEAL WITH DIFFERENT TYPES OF CLIENTS

by Robert Bowen

IN BUSINESS, BEING able to read people and quickly get a sense of who you're dealing with is an invaluable skill. It turns your encounter with a client into an opportunity to catch a glimpse of the upcoming project and how it will need to be handled. It is one of the building blocks of a professional relationship.

In today's digital age, the arena has shifted to the Web, and the online office space that most freelancers inhabit limits personal interaction. Though sussing out a client's personality via online communication is difficult, it remains an invaluable tool in your arsenal.

In the freelancing field, *you will encounter a range of client types*. Being able to *identify* which type you are dealing with allows you to develop the *right strategy* to maximize your interactions with them, and it could save your sanity. Following is a list of the most common personality types, the tell-tale signs that will tip you off, and suggestions on how to handle each type.

THE PASSIVE-AGGRESSIVE CLIENT

This is the client who is very passive when you ask for initial input, but when you submit the finished product, they aggressively attack it, demanding a lot of detailed changes, both major and minor. They had an idea of what they wanted all along but kept it mostly to themselves. Even though they showed appreciation of certain ideas and elements throughout the development process, do not expect the passive-aggressive client to keep any of them as they send revisions your way.

IDENTIFYING CHARACTERISTICS

- Communication is mostly one-sided and unhelpful during project development.
- Makes statements such as:
  - "I'm not really sure what we're looking for."
  - "Just do something that would appeal to us generally."
  - "You totally missed the point of what we wanted."

HOW TO DEAL WITH IT

Patience is key. Expecting the last-minute requests for revisions may soften the blow of the client's aggressive behavior. Keep your original layered design intact so that you can easily refine and change it later (not that you wouldn't, but it does happen). Also, make sure your contract specifies a limited number of revisions.

THE FAMILY FRIEND

This is the client whom you have known for years either through personal or family interaction, and this connection has landed you the job. The relationship will be tested and perhaps marred forever by what could very well be a nightmare of a project. This family friend believes he deserves a "special" price and unbridled access to your work. They will sometimes unwittingly belittle your work or not take it seriously because of their personal connection to you.

IDENTIFYING CHARACTERISTICS

- These clients are easy to identify because . . . well, you know them.
- Makes such statements as:
  - "Could you just throw something together for me?"
  - "I don't want you to think that just because I know you I want you to cut me a deal."
  - "You're going to charge me what?! But we go way back!"

HOW TO DEAL WITH IT

The way to deal with these clients depends on how well you know them and how much you value your relationship with them. But remember that anyone who would take advantage of such a relationship is not truly a friend, so respond accordingly. An honest approach could end up saving the relationship. But start off with a professional, not personal, tone, and they may follow your lead. Of course, if you truly value the relationship, you may want to pass on the job altogether.

THE UNDER-VALUER

Like the family friend, this client devalues your creative contributions. But there is a difference: you do not actually know this person. There is no rationale for their behavior. They feel they should get a "friend's" pricing rate not because they want to be friends with you, but because they do not see your work as being worth that much… even if they couldn't do it themselves. Not coming from a creative background or even having had exposure to the arts can mar someone's appreciation of the work that you do. After years in our field, we make it look easy, and that is what the under-valuer sees.

IDENTIFYING CHARACTERISTICS

- Does not respond to questions in a timely fashion.
- Makes such statements as:
  - "It's not like it takes much effort on your part."
  - "Couldn't you just throw something together for me?"
  - "How hard can this really be?"

HOW TO DEAL WITH IT

Confidence is key here. You know what your work demands and how well you do your job. The under-valuer will recognize this confidence. Don't back down or concede a point to the client when discussing your role in the project. Standing firm will establish the professional and respectful tone you deserve. If the client does not respond in kind, cut your losses and decline their project.

THE NITPICKER

This client is never fully satisfied with the work you do and constantly picks on minor details here and there that they dislike and want changed. Do not be surprised if they ask you to change these same details over and over ad nauseam. It is not a sign of disrespect (as it is with the other clients), but simply the nature of the person. They may have been burned in some other project and are now unsatisfied with everything in their path, including your work.

IDENTIFYING CHARACTERISTICS

- Complains almost constantly about unrelated things.
- Personal outlook comes with a scathing bite.
- Makes such statements as:
  - "How hard is it really to [fill in the blank with any rant]?"
  - "I'm not sure about this element here. It just doesn't pop!"
  - "I don't think you're really getting it."

HOW TO DEAL WITH IT

Once again, patience is important (especially if you have some sadistic reason for taking on nit-picking clients). Try to detach yourself from the project as much as possible, so that the constant nit-pickery does not affect you personally. It is easy to feel hurt or get defensive when your work is repeatedly questioned, and you may begin to doubt your skill. But understand that this is not about you or your talent; it is simply a personality trait of the person you are dealing with. And once again, protect yourself in the contract.

THE SCORNFUL SAVER

This client has similarities to the nit-picker and under-valuer but is actually impressed with your work and skill set. They criticize you merely to undermine your confidence in an attempt to lower your pricing rate. Unlike some other client types, the scornful saver understands creative people and their processes. But they are cheap and manipulative, and their scheme may have worked in their favor once or twice in the past. So, they continue to subtly abuse the people they hire in the hope of saving every last penny.

IDENTIFYING CHARACTERISTICS

- Compliments always come with a less-than-flattering qualifier.
- Takes time to respond to questions, sometimes making you ask more than once.
- Makes such statements as:
  - "I really like what you've done overall, but I'm unsure about one or two things."
  - "You may not have gotten exactly what we're looking for, but you're close."

HOW TO DEAL WITH IT

Once again, it is all about confidence. Having a solid understanding of your field and being confident in your knowledge and abilities will keep this client's manipulation in check. Standing your ground and even calling the client on some of their tactics could shift the balance of power over to you. Be prepared to walk away from the project if the disrespect and manipulation continues. There will be other projects and other clients.

THE "I-COULD-DO-THIS-MYSELF"-ER

Where to begin . . . When this client farms a project out to you, they make clear to you that they know how to do what they're hiring you to do but they just don't have the time to actually do it. They may be working at a firm or as an entrepreneur; either way, you are there to pick up their slack. If they're at a firm, you could be in for an interesting situation; they were likely hired for their particular style and proposals, and now you will have to please two sets of people: the person who hired you and the people who hired him.

IDENTIFYING CHARACTERISTICS

- Will generally be (or look) hectic and rushed.
- Communication from them often takes the form of short bursts of information.
- Makes such statements as:
  - "I could easily handle this if my schedule weren't so full."
  - "Really? Not sure that's the direction I would've gone in, but whatever."
  - "Remember, you are filling my shoes, and they're pretty big."

HOW TO DEAL WITH IT

The "I-Could-Do-This-Myself"-er will likely have recognized your talent and skill right away, which is why they hired you. They merely want you to know that this project (and thus you) is not above their ability. And though these reminders will grate on you periodically, they will let you run with your ideas, perhaps offering suggestions or feedback on the final design.

THE CONTROL FREAK

This client desperately needs to micro-manage every little detail of the project, no matter their qualifications. No decision may be made without their explicit input and approval. This tiresome person forces himself into your workflow, heedless of either invitation or protest, and demands access to you at whim. The concepts of boundaries and strict work processes are easily lost on the control freak, who constantly disrupts the flow. They may also believe you lack dedication or preparedness, further reinforcing their need to interfere.

IDENTIFYING CHARACTERISTICS

- Initial contact is long, detailed and one-sided, with little input sought from you.
- Your input remains unsought as the project pushes forward.
- Makes such statements as:
  - "This way we can keep in contact 24/7 in case you have any questions, or I do."
  - "I really know best what is right for the project and what is not."
  - "What do you mean, I'm distracting you? I am the only thing keeping this project on track!"

HOW TO DEAL WITH IT

If you absolutely must take on this client, for whatever reason, resign yourself to the fact that you will not be steering at any point. You will have to detach yourself from the work because you will have no control at all. You will merely be constructing, not designing, so just let go and let it happen. You may want to exclude this project from your portfolio.

THE DREAM CLIENT

This client, widely dismissed as a myth, does in fact exist and understands the full scope and artistry of your work. They value your role and creative contributions and want you in the driver's seat as soon as the project gets underway. They are timely with responses and payments . . . payments that they did not "negotiate" but rather accepted for what they are. They reflect on your suggestions and have confidence in your capabilities.

IDENTIFYING CHARACTERISTICS

- Is enthusiastic about the project and your involvement in it.
- Communication shows awareness of and respect for your role.
- Makes such statements as:
  - "Here's the brief we prepared. The rest is pretty much up to you."
  - "We like what we've seen and trust you'll do great things for us."

HOW TO DEAL WITH IT

Don't brag! Just enjoy the ride and hold on to them for as long as you possibly can!

WRAP-UP

Being able to identify the type of client you are dealing with will prepare you for the job ahead. It will also help you decide whether to accept the job in the first place. Your contract will reflect the power dynamics of the project, so the more you know about the client, the better able you will be to adjust the contract as necessary.

Robert Bowen is an emerging author, celebrated podcaster, and poet, and most recently the co-founder and imaginative co-contributor of the creative design and blogging duo at the Arbenting Freebies Blog and Dead Wings Designs.

10

HOW TO IMPROVE DESIGNER-CLIENT RELATIONSHIPS

by Aaron Griffith

GOOD BUSINESS RELATIONSHIPS rarely "just happen." While a smitten designer and her starry-eyed client may start out well with a "honeymoon" of a successful initial project launch, things can get rocky fast. The once-anticipated phone calls requesting new designs that used to be welcomed are now dreaded, and the previously infrequent and brief revision requests are now hostile diatribes critiquing every aspect of a submitted project.

Truly, if you thought that hearing "Let's just be friends" from your junior high love interest was bad, wait until one of your clients cancels your project with an email that ends with "One of our sales guys bought that Photoshopper thing; he's going to give this logo stuff a shot."

Just like a romantic relationship, client/designer partnerships take work to be successful. While each client has his own unique needs, here are a few tips to help keep your working relationships healthy and enjoyable.

DON'T BE AFRAID TO SAY "NO"

This may seem counterintuitive, but you certainly can have too many clients that require way more time and effort than they are worth. If you have the time, energy, and manpower at your disposal, then by all means take on new projects and grow your business. However, if you don't have these limited resources (and they are limited!), don't place an unneeded burden on yourself or your team to pull an excellent final product out of thin air. If you over-commit yourself you run the risk of not spending the time and effort needed on existing work, making your current clients unhappy and potentially driving them away. It can be very tempting to obligate yourself to new projects that could be enjoyable or lucrative for you and your team, but if you know that you can't handle the work at that moment, it is far better to say "no" than to risk your reputation and good name. At best, you will either hand the project in late or you will overwork yourself and your team while sacrificing time on existing work; neither is desirable. Far better to politely decline a request and ask for a rain check — the prospective client will respect you for it and potentially come calling later.

On a related note (and keeping with the relationship theme), sometimes a "divorce" is called for between yourself and a client. If you find that one client is taking up most of your time, causing most of your headaches, and could easily be replaced by someone better, the time may be right to move on. A decision like this should never be made lightly, but it can potentially make your life easier and open up space for better customers.

TALK THINGS OUT

A lot of problems in a romantic relationship can be avoided if both parties are willing to admit that they aren't mind readers who intuitively understand the needs of the other person. The same goes for designers and their clients: no matter how well a designer thinks they understand a client's instructions, they likely are missing something because the client either doesn't think that they need certain information or they assume that such info is a given. By simply asking a few pointed questions to your clients, you can stimulate necessary discussion that will do away with uncertainties that lead to unnecessary revisions and wasted time. Here are a few examples:

- What is the ultimate purpose of this design?
- Who are you trying to reach with the design?
- How will this design be used (flyer, website, billboard, etc.)?
- How much time should I spend on this/ how much money are you willing to spend?

Also, if you anticipate any potential conflict or difficulties that will arise with your client while you work on a project for them, negotiate the details before starting work. In many cases negotiation may mean letting them know that you require a certain amount of freedom in your work to make their design a success. To have a reference point for future discussions, write down all the agreements that you and your client come to in your negotiations. Ultimately, you need to make sure that you understand as much as you can about who your client is and what they expect from you before you start work. While talking things out at length beforehand may seem tedious, trying to work solely off of your intuition won't get you very far and it likely won't endear you to your clients.

CREATE A WORK PROCESS

Creative types typically eschew uniformity and predictability, but the implementation of a standardized (read: boring) work process might be just what you need to improve relationships with your clients. Yes, "process" has the connotations of an overused piece of management-speak, but what is it really? Simply put, it is a standardized way that you organize your thoughts and work so that you can work more efficiently and effectively. Your process doesn't have to be too specific or detailed, but it should touch on every aspect of starting, working on, and delivering your project to a client.

What does a process look like? Here's a general example. Upon receiving a project request:

1. Confirm project details (due date, cost, etc.).
2. Task out every aspect of the project.
3. Figure out what tasks are yours; delegate others with specific instructions.
4. Create a draft for review.
5. Solicit feedback from the client.
6. Make adjustments based on feedback. (Repeat steps 5 and 6 as needed.)
7. Bill the customer.
8. Check back in six months for more projects.

You may think that something as simple as this plan is unnecessary, and you may be right. However, it can be very helpful to have an ordered checklist of tasks that you always do to refer to when working with clients. Having a process checklist like this hanging on your wall can give you direction and keep you on track when managing multiple or complex projects. Better yet, one idea might be to even share your process with your client — that way you can point them to the specific step that you are on in your work for them. A client will appreciate knowing exactly what is going on with the project, and they will be less likely to badger you with requests for status updates.

GET "PREEMPTIVE" FEEDBACK

Before you asked your middle school crush out on a date, you probably ran your game plan by your friends and had them look for flaws ("Dude, you should definitely not take her to Burger King and then *Schindler's List!*"). Similarly, there are few things that can be more helpful than having other people look over your design work and critique it before you submit it to a client. However, getting good, actionable feedback isn't always easy and it can be a very humbling process. Here are two tips for those who want to get preemptive input from others:

- *Get feedback from the right people.* Not all criticism is created equal. Some of it is really valuable, some is average, and the rest could get you fired if you implemented it. Therefore, you need to choose your feedback sources carefully. However, this doesn't mean that you should only solicit help from other designers or professionals in your field. It is essential to get an outsider's perspective that comes from someone in your client's target market, or at least other designers that understand the population that you are trying to cater to.

- *Put your ego aside.* Getting your work critiqued by others can be a painful process, especially if you put lots of time and energy into your projects and you take pride in what you do. However, if you really want good feedback, be prepared to have your design ideas called into question. Don't be defensive or view critiques as ad hominem attacks on you or your philosophy as a designer. Try to remember that your work isn't ultimately about you — it`s a service for someone else and their needs as a client. Once you do this you are lessening the emotional burden on yourself, thus making it easier to hear and implement suggestions from others regarding your work.

BE TIMELY

You wouldn't show up 30 minutes late for a first date, and regular tardiness can be a constant source of aggravation for some significant others. It's not too different with your design work; be on time, and nerves are much less likely to be frayed. Being timely sounds simple (and it is), but it is essential that designers understand that nothing peeves a client like turning projects in late or missing set deadlines. The key to being on time has a lot to do with staying focused on your work, doing what you say you will do, and not stretching yourself too thin (see the first tip). But perhaps the best strategy for working with your client in a timely manner is to stay in constant communication with them. This may mean giving a regularly scheduled update on the project's progress, or it may just require the occasional email or phone call to let them informally know how things are going. Choosing how to do this is up to you, but the main reason for doing so is to keep your client aware of any issues or problems that you run into that would prevent you from handing in a project on time. Most clients will have no problem pushing back a due date because of unforeseen circumstances as long as they are kept in the loop with what is going on and they are made aware of problems when they happen. Explaining an unexpected issue two weeks (or even two days) from the due date is much easier than two hours before the project was due.

CONCLUSION

Hopefully this article has given you some helpful advice in successfully improving and maintaining your relationships with clients (with a few dating pointers along the way, free of charge!). This list isn't exhaustive — there are many different strategies to build rapport with your clients — but just starting with these five basic practices will strengthen the relationships you currently have and build a solid foundation for starting new ones.

Aaron Griffith is marketing project manager for Air Cycle Corporation and LampRecycling. Both companies provide recycling and other green solutions for businesses and large organizations all over the world.

11

HOW TO COMMUNICATE EFFECTIVELY WITH DEVELOPERS

by Ryan Scherf

IF YOU HAVE ever worked with a developer or a development team, this article will probably strike close to home. As designers, we work with dozens of developers across the globe at length in terms of what needs to be accomplished with the user interface, and what is required to make this happen. Often, however, we find developers with whom we don't see eye to eye.

When many people are involved in a project, it is important to make sure that they have a common understanding of the problem and its solution. This is not meant as a slam on developers, as I believe they are a much different breed than designers; rather, the hope is that if you follow some of the principles outlined in this chapter, your development process can be streamlined a bit.

PROVIDE AN ADEQUATE LEVEL OF DOCUMENTATION

Modern software development methodologies may lead you to believe that less documentation is better; however this isn't always the case. For starters, the best documentation that is provided is the user interface. Not only does the UI show the developer where data should be and how it should be formatted, but it also represents the basic flow of what needs to happen. A well thought-out and complete UI will make you a developer's dream colleague. Granted, there will always be developers who don't like everything defined and love to take liberties with your interface. These developers are rare (and most of the time unwelcome) in the design community.

As a designer, you don't need to have every single page thought out before starting development, but it is helpful to stay ahead of the developers. Plan your features accordingly, and make sure you at least have some type of structure (HTML, etc.) ready to go when they need it. It is a lot easier for developers to come through on a polished page and insert data where it is needed than to create the page from scratch and have the designer come in after them.

BE DECISIVE

As designers, we make hundreds of decisions on each interface we work on. Whether it is the height of navigation, the amount of text in a table cell, or the alignment of text in the footer, we need to make many decisions every day. This is very similar to developers, who have just as many (or more) nitpicky decisions to make on every piece of functionality they write. But the beauty of development is that it is less subjective than design. Sure, the architecture, code style, and language could all be subject to opinion, but not in the way that design is subjective. Some people prefer stock images, while others illustrations. Everyone has a favorite color, while many colors may be perceived differently by every person.

As designers, we need to decide what the interface should look like. Although some developers may enjoy tinkering with the UI, it's not their job, and doing so ultimately slows them down from what they should be doing: developing.

It is also important to try not to change the design while the developer is in the middle of developing that specific feature. Agile and Scrum methodologies insist that the developers work with the requirements they have at the time, and in the following sprint, the developer can revisit the feature and make modifications. As designers, we should try to avoid any type of refactoring of the UI. It is tedious work for developers to go back and change HTML.

Choose an HTML structure and stick to it. Try to account for all potential design features in your first draft of the HTML (even if it makes your HTML seem somewhat bloated). CSS should already control the look of your interface, so try to think of HTML as backend code that is more difficult to change than a font color in CSS.

Developers dislike refactoring their code as much as we dislike providing revisions to clients. Get the "most perfect" result as soon as you can.

COMMUNICATION IS KEY, SO BE AVAILABLE

You have spent countless hours mocking up the UI, polishing it to your liking, and you're ready to hand it off to the development team. Often, this is where design ends and development begins. As designers, this is where we should be most involved to ensure that the design concept is fully realized in the working application. Avoid just "throwing the design over the fence" and hoping the developers implement it exactly as you have envisioned it in your mind.

It is also important to not disappear from the project at this point. At the least, be available by email so the developers can contact you about issues with your designs. Respond quickly to ensure your developers are staying on track with the final product. Once again, be decisive in your communication. Most of the time, the real data don't match what you mocked up, and there are many issues you will need to work out in conjunction with your developer.

AVOID FEATURE CREEP

The crew over at 37signals.com wrote a quite famous book, *Getting Real,* which talks about the problem of feature creep. This topic is probably more relevant to product managers, however it is also important for designers. Always ask yourself, "why does this feature matter?" Avoid a UI that is far too complex, as it only adds time to development, and ultimately forces you to miss deadlines. If you can't come up with a good reason why it should be included, then it doesn't need to be there. It will only slow your team down, as well as create more for you to support.

Focus on what is important for your users. For example, if your users aren't going to use invoicing heavily, don't spend your time on it. If you already know better alternatives to your features exist in the market, don't include your own.

As we developed one of our recent projects, we weren't planning on providing a full suite of tools that included invoicing. We wanted to concentrate on proposals, bids, and requests for proposals (RFPs), knowing that we still needed to serve a small user base that may require invoicing. We chose to add in a bare-bones system (simple line items, nothing recurring), because we felt it might be useful to some people who didn't already have an invoicing solution. We also realized that users probably wouldn't want to switch to our invoicing system (mainly because they already had a solution), so there was no sense in creating something robust.

AVOID SETTING UNREALISTIC DEADLINES

As designers, we can quickly turn around designs in a few days and be done with it. Unfortunately, this is not the case for development. The ratio of design to development hours is not even close to 1:1. Make sure your deadlines allow enough time for the developer to implement the features, as well as any back-and-forth time for questions.

No matter how hard you try to hit your deadlines, something always comes up. Perhaps another project, maybe kids or family commitments. Try your best not to announce any hard dates until you are absolutely sure you will hit them. Announce the week before (or even month before) if you feel comfortable. If you just started a project, never commit to launching in the next six months. It just won't happen, and your users may or may not hold you accountable for that date.

As irritating as missing deadlines is for you and your team, it's even more irritating for potential customers who are waiting for your app to change their workflow. Be vague about deadlines, and keep people wanting more.

TEST IT YOURSELF

Don't rely on your developers to write perfect code, as it will never happen. You can't always rely on developers to test their code to make sure it functions properly, fulfills requirements, and ultimately works in the manner you described. But remember: developers don't write buggy code on purpose. They would rather write perfect code and work on newer, cooler features each release. Since your developers are so close to the code and system, they will inevitably miss something. Don't blame them; help them fix it. Explain to them where it's failing and what the desired action should be.

Also, as you take on the testing, you free up the developer to keep moving on the backend, which once again, is where they should be focusing. And as you find bugs, make sure to fully document them, including screenshots, how to re-create them, and most importantly, the desired outcome.

Of all the developers we've worked with, none have been interested in any type of testing past in-the-code unit testing. Large enterprise shops hire entire Quality Assurance teams to follow-up on developers' work (which doesn't make it right, but it's the way it is). Help your developers out by testing their features — your app will be much better for it.

MEASURE PERFORMANCE

One last point is to measure performance. Set milestones and goals and make sure you are hitting your marks. Try to monitor how your team is doing on fixing bugs versus creating new features, as there will always be a snowball effect. Fix bugs early and often to prevent them from growing into larger and more complex bug colonies in the future.

Ryan Scherf is a freelance web designer, developer, and entrepreneur. When he isn't wasting the day away on Twitter, he can be found building his most recent venture, SixCentral, a client proposal organization and management application.

12

HOW TO EDUCATE YOUR CLIENTS ON WEB DEVELOPMENT

by Aurimas Adomavicius

IF YOU ARE running a design agency, your job is very likely to combine business development, graphic design, technology, and user experience design — a basketful of very different fields. When dealing with clients, you face the challenge of clearly and effectively communicating the goals and results of the work in all these areas. In this chapter, we provide you with some ideas on *sharing information and knowledge with developers and clients* — a couple of tips and tricks we've learned from our own experience.

As designers, our core purpose is to solve business challenges for our clients. No, I haven't forgotten you Mac-loving, single-mouse-button-fanatic designers. A business solution includes an application platform, solid data design, and a page design that makes the UI and website approachable and easy to use (for converting, transacting, clicking on a monkey's butt, etc.). Your daily challenge, then, is to deliver the project on time while satisfying the client's visual, business, and aesthetic requirements.

YOU'RE NOT AS SMART AS YOU THINK

I like to think that I'm always right, and that becomes tricky when communicating with clients. As a professional, I am able to detect patterns, usability issues, trends in the industry, and other important issues that the client might not be aware of. On the other hand, I'm a complete idiot when it comes to semi-conductor temperature tolerances, furniture for pre-school institutions, and the importance of steel spikes in lederhosen. My client, on the other hand, may be an *Encyclopedia Britannica* on every one of those topics. What I'm trying to say is that you have to remember that you're an expert only on your own field and that you should prick up your ears when the client tells you something.

NEGOTIATING FOR A WIN-WIN RESULT

So, as you tread your pitiable pixel-pushing existence, you should be aware of things that might give your sorry designer self an advantage in negotiating those sticking points in projects. Have you ever had a client who wanted a larger logo on their website? Maybe a logo done in Flash, with a spinning earth and sparkles!? All valid requirements, I'm sure; and so during that meeting, as you slowly reached for the pencil to stab your quads under the table, you should have realized that business owners love their brands and are emotionally attached to them. You should have based your response, then, on a composite of research-based facts (best presented as a link to a reputable source on the Web) — an explanation that is specific to their business.

> Client: I really want a bigger logo. I feel like it's getting lost in the website.
>
> You: I understand why your brand is important to you. I have research here based on the top 500 retailers on the Internet and their logo sizes. The research indicates that the logo should take up less space than or be similar in size to the call-to-action element, or be one-fourth of the website's width at most. In our case, that 'View products' link should be the focal point of the website.

DAMAGE CONTROL: GIVING IN IS PART OF THE JOB

A successful negotiator (and you are a negotiator — perhaps not a gun-toting, hostage-holding Samuel L. Jackson, but a negotiator nonetheless) delivers a solution that makes both parties win. Your client is happy that their demands were met by their responsive and well-informed developer, and you're happy because you didn't have to waste time in meetings. Hopefully, after you've demonstrated the facts and your reasoning for keeping the logo at the same size, the client will change his mind and leave you basking in the glory of being right and not having to go back for a fix. In case they don't, you still might not have to increase the size; perhaps you could reassess your use of white space or employ other visual trickery of that devilishly sexy design field.

POSITION OF AUTHORITY: YOUR VOICE MUST BE HEARD

As I mentioned, you do wield some authority in this line of work, but your client does also in their business. I recommend that for every project, you establish attainable and clearly defined goals, goals that will be measured by the website's performance and enforced by strict deadlines. If you or your client doesn't meet certain goals or deliverables by the deadlines, you could still launch the website if all critical items are completed, and then clear up the remaining items once the website is live. This strategy is used by major tech companies such as Google and accomplishes several important things:

- Forces you to deliver on time
- Focuses you on date-based deliverables, which makes the client easier to educate on "sticky" issues
- Forces the client to deliver content, stock photos, and their ideas to you on time, because any missing features would have to be paid for on an hourly consulting basis

As you work toward these goals, know that at a certain point your opinion and decisions are critical to the project's success. There's no backing down or hiding your tail between your legs. Sometimes you cannot negotiate, and the client must understand that they are paying you for a reason: because you know your stuff!

Keep in mind that your client also has authority and knowledge that might not be apparent to you during negotiations. For example:

> Client: We want IE6 support through the website. The website will have a lot of JavaScript, dynamic elements, PNG graphics, etc.
>
> You: [Jotting down a reminder to send hate mail to the IE6 team at Microsoft,] IE6 is actually an outdated browser that has security flaws, a very poor rendering engine, and very few users out there. I recommend we don't accommodate it (even Mailchimp doesn't!), and we tell those suckers to go to hell.
>
> Client: Did I mention that we service a large restaurant industry, and a lot of the terminals in restaurants still run Windows XP with IE6?
>
> You: [Updates reminder to hunt down IE6's creators.]

At the end of the day you are at the mercy of the client, and you need to meet all of his requirements. But you also have to recognize your value and be able to demonstrate it through examples, research, and logical arguments.

Be responsive: ask a lot of questions in order to understand the client's motivation. I endorse client education, but not to the point of losing the client and project. Remember that your client is a resource to you, and good communication will enable both of you to complete the project in time to watch the men's figure-skating competition.

Aurimas Adomavicius is the creative lead at DevBridge, a Chicago-based web application development company. He is also responsible for the creation of the website review community Concept Feedback. A photographer, web developer, and web designer, his opinion can be often heard on the company blog and on Twitter.

13

HOW TO EXPLAIN TO CLIENTS THAT THEY ARE WRONG

by Sam Barnes

GIFS OF SPINNING @ symbols on the "Contact us" page. Common usability mistakes for the sake of visual appeal. Splash pages. Fancy search box. No whitespace. Music on page load. Home page banner of a jigsaw-puzzle globe with a piece missing. Sometimes you just know that *what a client is requesting is wrong and that you have to find a way to tell them*. But how?

IS THE CLIENT WRONG?

Before getting into how to explain to a client that they're wrong, ask yourself, "Is the client wrong to begin with?" Just because you don't approve of the direction they're taking or of a request they've made doesn't necessarily mean it is not a step in the right direction for the project. To be able to answer this question effectively, you need to train yourself to be completely objective and humble when dealing with client requests.

First, appreciate one critical thing: the client probably knows her target audience a lot better than you do. Just as Web professionals quickly learn personality types among their own clients, your client interacts with her target audience on a daily basis and knows what makes them tick . . . and that may be just what makes you cringe.

You can begin to establish whether the client is wrong simply by exploring why the client is making such a request and what the business case for it is. It could well be a situation in which the client spoke to many people in the target audience demographic, and they all said that they were more likely to click an animated Flash banner link than a static one, or that they felt more engaged by a website that had stock images of smiling people everywhere.

It could be that the picture of the jigsaw-puzzle globe with a piece missing actually sums up the client's sales pitch quite well and that similar messaging has proven to win over potential customers in the past.

Of course, when faced with such a situation, a good Web professional would understand the business driver and suggest alternative solutions that convey the same message and achieve the same goal but that are unique, original, and creative.

Whatever the case, though, always keep an open mind. Don't assume the client is wrong before seeing the evidence. One guarantee in this business is that the more you design and develop websites, the more often you'll find yourself in situations where, six months after a project's launch, you hear that the most positive feedback from users wasn't the cool bit of JavaScript you implemented using groundbreaking technology, but rather something that you considered boring and unoriginal but that excited the client during development. We deliver websites for the client's target audience, not our peers in the Web community: sometimes painful to swallow, but always true.

That scenario aside, let's put our cool hats on again and assume that the request for the jigsaw-puzzle globe has come in, and that it clearly has nothing to do with the client's business, and that it has made you curl up in a corner of the room, banging your head against the wall, muttering "Why? Why? Why?"

What approaches can you take to explain to the client that, in your professional opinion, they're wrong?

SPEAK THE CLIENT'S LANGUAGE

One of the most common problems, especially among freelancers, is an inability to speak the client's language. Being able to speak in a way that relates to the client's business sense is crucial at all stages of managing a Web project, but never more so than when challenging a client's decision.

If you're trying to explain to a client that a rotating banner (or any other feature) may not be the most effective use of their budget, rather than say something like, "I just don't think it will work," or "I'm not sure you have the budget," ask instead how they think implementing it will benefit their business, generate more quality leads, or increase conversions.

Always emphasize the main goals, or KPIs (key performance indicators), of the project. You'd be surprised by how often such a question will result in a few seconds of uncomfortable silence, as the client realizes that they want the feature because they think it looks cool, when in fact they can't connect it to a KPI.

Building a website or Web application should be treated in the same way as growing a business:

1. Know what you want to achieve.
2. Define some measurable KPIs or goals.
3. Develop a plan.
4. Begin executing the plan.
5. Evaluate every decision along the way to make sure it supports a KPI, thus taking repeated steps toward achieving the project's goals.

By maintaining this approach, you will also radically change the client's opinion of you, from that of a creative hippie-type to a business-savvy Web designer or developer whom they should listen to if they want to stay focused on the purpose of the project.

Being able to speak the client's language will undoubtedly help greatly when the time comes to tell the client that she's wrong. Beyond using Buzzword Bingo words with confidence, you need to be able to back them up with valuable advice drawn from your area of specialization.

ESTABLISH YOURSELF AS THE EXPERT

One of the most important ways to make the ordeal of explaining to a client that they're wrong as stress-free as possible for both parties is to establish that you are the Web expert. If you do this, the client will completely trust you and your recommendations without a moment's hesitation.

But even if you are a Web expert, the position is not always easy to establish, because it usually only becomes apparent over time, after you've gotten a few successful decisions or projects under your belt with the client. It doesn't help either that many clients still regard creative digital agencies and freelancers as either kids living in their parents' basement or shady professionals out to take them for every last penny.

Though a challenge, you can establish your credibility quickly using a few methods, some of which are relatively simple to implement.

BE PROFESSIONAL

Before they're convinced that you're a digital professional and that they should trust your recommendations, you must first demonstrate your professionalism by doing the basics well:

- Be punctual at meetings and teleconferences.
- Always speak in a professional manner.
- Deliver pre-sales paperwork on time.
- Present all documents and images on professionally branded templates.
- Use correct grammar and punctuation in emails.

You'd be surprised by how quickly clients pick up on deficiencies in these basic business skills. Their perception of you and your recommendations will be immediately affected. Unless you come across as the consummate professional early on, shaking off this reputation will be difficult.

DON'T BE SHY ABOUT CITING HIGH-PROFILE CLIENTS

You could well be a digital guru who has spent years working in the industry and earned the respect of the Web community, but most clients won't understand what this means. They have never heard of websites such as Smashing Magazine or magazines such as .Net, and they probably won't grasp the gravitas that comes with being a speaker at Web conferences such as SXSW.

However, all clients tend to respond when you say you have worked on a high-profile brand website. When clients hear that you've been hired by a big name that they've heard of and whose products they perhaps use, they sit up like a meerkat and think they've hit the jackpot. Simples!

While some Web folk aren't always comfortable selling themselves, and while big brand experience is not always proof of ability, it almost always resonates with clients and makes them see you as more credible. This reinforces your position as an expert whose advice should be heeded. After all, if big brand X thought you were good, you must be, right?

Sometimes, of course, no matter how much credibility you demonstrate, a client may choose not to listen to your recommendations. But perhaps they'll listen to others . . .

BACK UP RECOMMENDATIONS WITH EVIDENCE

How often in life have you volunteered your point of view to someone for months, only to be beaten down each time; and yet when someone else comes into the picture and says the exact same thing, their advice is seized upon as revolutionary? This is human nature and happens just as much when explaining to clients that they're wrong.

If a client is, for whatever reason, unpersuaded by your arguments, you might want to consider producing evidence that backs up your recommendations.

This evidence can come in many forms. For example:

- Blog posts from world-respected Web experts
- Statistics from large usability studies
- Well-known cases where the same thing was tried and had negative results

This kind of evidence is obvious. But sometimes, the less obvious kind can be just as effective:

- Guerrilla usability testing, by asking the client to obtain feedback from employees within the company
- Using free tools like Flash to test designs
- Submitting designs to communities dedicated to providing design feedback
- Feedback from customers with whom the client has a good relationship
- Setting up a poll on the website that presents both ideas
- Web analytics from the current website

Common points of contention will be which browsers to support, which screen resolutions to optimize for, and where to put the fold. But no matter the debate, backing up your point of view with trusted third parties can sometimes tip the balance in your favor and improve how the client perceives your dedication, enthusiasm, and passion for getting it right.

SOMETIMES BEING DIRECT WORKS

When all else fails, you could always tell the client flat out that they're wrong. This is always a risky move, because clients will react differently. Some will appreciate it, while others will find it disrespectful or personally insulting.

But if you feel strongly about it and you've tried every other method, being direct might do the trick.

Personally, I've been in situations in which I've had no alternative but to tell a client that their request is "naff." To my surprise, despite the ferocity with which the client initially defended their opinion, they backed down immediately and thanked me, saying that this is what they were paying me for: to be strong and stubborn and to tell them things like this. However, merely saying that something is naff and nothing more is not ideal; you have to offer an alternative solution.

Use this approach with caution. Take into account your rapport with the client, and be passive in your tone of voice. Also, choose your method of communication wisely; for example, being so direct by email is usually a big mistake because of the possibility of misinterpretation.

If possible, be direct with the client face to face or by telephone. This allows you to deliver the message directly and set the right tone. You will also be able to observe the client's body language or hear their response instantly and then quickly adjust your approach if needed. Generally, if a client turns green with fury, their nostrils emit a trace of steam, and their clothes rip at the seams, you may want to back down and move swiftly to the next item on the agenda . . . or call an ambulance because they may be ill.

Of course, sometimes no matter what you say or do, a client will overrule and insist that you follow their request. You know what? That's okay. It happens. That's life.

But that doesn't necessarily have to be the end of the debate!

KNOW WHEN AND HOW TO ADMIT DEFEAT

Occasionally you'll try every known method of explaining to a client that they're wrong, and nothing works. They'll continue insisting that you design or develop whatever they want or else they'll go to someone who will. And yet you feel with complete sincerity that they're making a mistake that will have a negative impact on their business. This is never a good situation to be in.

There really are no hard and fast rules on what to do in such a situation. Each case should be treated on its own basis. But with experience comes the instinct of knowing when to admit defeat and do as you're told.

This feeling is never nice, but sometimes that's how it is. And if you have to sit in the corner and be quiet, do it professionally and politely. Under no circumstances should you throw your toys out of the stroller and give the client attitude. Simply explain to them that you have put forward your recommendations and given your reasons. At the end of the day, it's their business and their decision. It stings, but you've done all you can, and your dignity remains intact. But don't give up yet!

TREAT DEFEAT AS AN OPPORTUNITY

Saying that good entrepreneurs view every defeat as an opportunity is almost a cliché these days. But it's true, and these situations are no different. There's admitting defeat, and then there's pretending to admit defeat! Once you've been beaten down by a client, accept it, get over it, and think positively about how you can turn defeat into a win/win for everyone.

For example, suggest to the client that if they choose to press ahead against your recommendation, then your next recommendation will be to implement some custom Web analytics to monitor the outcome of the decision.

If a client insists on giving the home page banner a small call to action that, in your opinion, is difficult to read or not prominent enough, persuade them to let you implement some A/B testing: one month with their banner and one month with your proposed solution, and let the statistics do the talking. No client would continue to insist on their solution if yours delivered a better return on investment.

(If you're thinking, "What the heck is A/B testing?" even better! This is an ideal opportunity to learn a valuable skill while getting paid and giving your client excellent service!)

SUMMARY

Explaining to a client that they're wrong is never easy. It could blow up in your face and damage what was a good relationship. But everyone is wrong sometimes, and clients are no different. Always start by asking yourself if the client is, in fact, wrong. Or are you trying to impose your opinion (based on a narrow Web-only view) on what is ultimately a business decision that affects the client's entire strategy, both online and offline?

If you conclude that their direction is still misguided, open a dialogue with them in language they relate too: business language. Rather than say it won't work, ask them what goals or return on investment they think the direction will help achieve.

Establish yourself as the digital expert from the moment you make contact with the client by conducting all aspects of your work with professionalism. Do everything you can to position yourself as someone who has the experience to suggest alternative solutions. And where possible, back up your recommendations with third-party material and user feedback.

If all else fails, be direct with the client. But know which clients you can be direct with and when you will have to back down. Finally, don't let being overruled be the end of the debate. Suggest testing periods, and let the web analytics do the talking. All clients respond when they see important metrics go up rather than down!

Sam Barnes is the Web Project Manager at Rawnet. Although a little short for a Stormtrooper, he can be found posting articles at thesambarnes.com, a blog dedicated to the subject of web project management.

14

HOW TO RESPOND EFFECTIVELY TO DESIGN CRITICISM

by Andrew Follett

WINSTON CHURCHILL ONCE said: "Criticism may not be agreeable, but it is necessary. It fulfills the same function as pain in the human body. It calls attention to an unhealthy state of things." Regardless of where you work or who you work for, being able to take criticism is part of the job description. Whether you're getting feedback from your boss or a client, having a proper perspective on criticism and a sound understanding of how to use it effectively is important.

Unfortunately, not many people enjoy criticism. In fact, many have developed a thick skin and take pride in their ability to brush it off and move on. However, despite its negative connotation, criticism often presents excellent opportunities to grow as a designer. Before you can respond effectively, you need to understand what those opportunities are.

Let's look at some important aspects of getting constructive criticism:

- *Uncover blind spots:* Doing your own thing is easy, but your habits will eventually become deeply ingrained and hard to break. Criticism gives you a vital outside perspective on your work, uncovering potential areas for improvement that you are unable to see by yourself.
- *Challenge yourself:* Feedback challenges you to be a better designer. Rather than settle for your own standards, you are pushed to take your work to the next level.

- *Develop communication skills:* If nothing else, dealing with a critic can dramatically improve the way you communicate — an essential skill for any successful design career.

- *Outside motivation:* Constructive criticism often gives you the kick in the butt you need to learn a new design skill or technique. Self-motivation is great, but everyone could use a hand from time to time.

- *A lesson in humility:* Never underestimate the importance of humility. Although criticism can bruise the ego, it keeps you grounded, making you easier to work with and more open to learning from others.

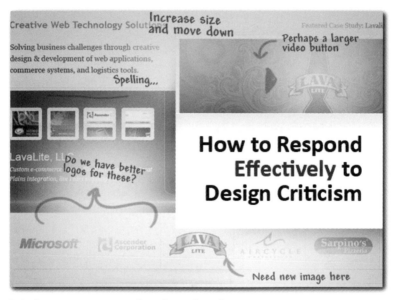

Think of criticism as an opportunity for professional growth.

A positive view of criticism isn't enough. You also need to know how to respond effectively when it comes. Here are eight tips you can use to start making the most of criticism today.

HAVE THE RIGHT ATTITUDE

Design is subjective and, like any art form, has no rulebook. No one can tell you what is "right" and "wrong" with your work, but that doesn't mean you can completely ignore your boss's or client's opinion either. However, by taking criticism and feedback with the right attitude, you can use it to your advantage and even enjoy it.

Everyone looks at design through a filter shaped by personal experience, and others' filters are usually very different from your own. While you may have a degree in design and 10 years of experience, not everyone will agree with your "expert" opinion, so don't expect them to. The important thing is to have a proper attitude from the beginning. Expect others to disagree with you, and be open to new perspectives. Align your expectations and understand that criticism is part of the process. While harsh criticism can cut deep and even scar, it can also motivate, instruct, and do all of the good things mentioned earlier.

Last, but not least, try to remove yourself from the criticism and view it as a commentary on your actions or work and not as a personal attack. While easier said than done, this distinction is key to responding effectively. If you can rise above the criticism and respond calmly and effectively, you will not only earn the admiration of your critic but feel better doing it. Set the right expectations, understand the benefits, remove yourself from the equation, and remember, attitude truly is everything.

CLARIFY THE OBJECTIVE

Clearly identifying the goal of a design before you share it with others is always a good idea. Are you showing it off to mom for some fridge time? Is it a client who's trying to solve a business challenge through design? Or perhaps you're consulting a friend with no experience or stake in the project.

Regardless, a vague or confused objective will always elicit off-target feedback, so make sure everyone involved "gets it" before taking action. To respond effectively to criticism, you need to be sure that the critic understands your goals. Be specific. Present your objective in clear and concise terms; the criticism you receive will be targeted and actionable as a result.

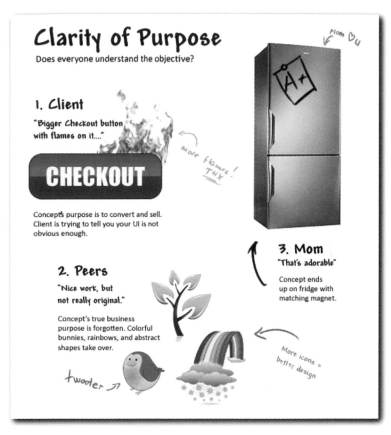

Clarify your objective for your audience to ensure useful feedback.

CHECK YOUR FIRST REACTION

For most people (me included), the first reaction to criticism is to get defensive or even lash out. If this sounds like you, take time to develop the habit of taking a deep breath and counting to 10 before responding. This simple yet effective method gives you a chance to regain composure and allow logic to prevail over emotion. The last thing you want to do is get overly emotional and give a response that you will later regret. Remember, in most cases, your critic is only trying to help you.

Despite the initial sting, you need honest feedback to become a better designer. This is especially important for enthusiasts or beginners in the trade. All visual arts have an intrinsic reward mechanism: the more you create, the more you sense the progression of your skill.

It's a loop that keeps all artists going, and when this euphoric moment is crushed by accurate and much-needed criticism, recovering may be difficult. Keep in mind, though, that your skill and perceptiveness in this field will mature over time. If you have the right attitude to begin with, the proper response will follow.

SEPARATE THE WHEAT FROM THE CHAFF

Unfortunately, not all criticism is constructive. Some people are in a bad mood, bitter, or just plain negative and will take any chance to put others down. Some are also inexperienced or unqualified to give you valuable feedback. While design is subjective, being able to separate useful feedback from cheap shots and misinformation is important. However, this is not an excuse to ignore comments that you don't like. Unless you believe a critique was given in malice or ignorance, don't be quick to dismiss it.

Here are a few tips to distinguish between the two:

- *Specific:* Valuable feedback is always specific. It is clear, logical and defined. "The logo is ugly" or "I don't like the color choice" are examples of useless criticism (if you get a lot of this, see the "Dig Deeper When Necessary" section below).
- *Actionable:* Constructive criticism should enable you to take immediate action. You should come away with a clearer idea of how to improve the concept and the path to follow.
- *Objective:* Useful feedback is unbiased. It gives you a unique perspective without an ulterior motive. Objective criticism will always be even-tempered and appropriate.

LEARN FROM IT

This step is possibly the hardest one in this learning experience but by far the most important. For criticism to serve its purpose, you need to act on it! Don't just go back to business as usual; make an effort to improve. The great thing about criticism is that it uncovers our blind spots, weaknesses that only others can see. When you're confronted by criticism, don't let the opportunity pass: write it down and do whatever it takes to change for the better.

If someone criticizes your copywriting skills, start with baby steps. Read a relevant blog once a week. Buy a book. Practice writing headlines for 10 minutes each day. Small victories are often the quickest path to success. Eventually you will improve and have your critic to thank.

Use criticism productively to improve your efforts.

LOOK FOR A NEW IDEA

If you can't learn anything new, look for a new idea. A different perspective gives you a chance to examine your work from a viewpoint that you would never have considered otherwise. Just as you get inspiration from a gallery or another talented designer, you can find ideas and inspiration in constructive criticism; seeing it just requires you to step back. Be curious, and approach the criticism objectively; it could be incredibly useful.

Criticism is sometimes the cold shower you need to wake up and hit the "Reset" button on a project. Remember, your work is based on your own preconceived notions of what the client wants, and you should always be open to the possibility that you have missed the mark. In the event that you do need to start over, discuss the objectives and expectations right away. Clarifying this information in the first place might have prevented a re-do altogether.

DIG DEEPER WHEN NECESSARY

At some point, everyone has received vague, unclear, or unactionable feedback. It's a part of life. Unfortunately, unless you take the initiative, this type of feedback is useless to everyone involved. However, if you're willing to dig a little deeper, you may uncover things that no one else was willing to tell you. Start by asking open-ended questions that get to the core of the issue, questions like, "I want to understand your point of view. Could you please provide more detail?" or "How can I improve?" Ask for specifics and, above all else, honesty. These kinds of questions will help keep communication lines open and allow you to walk away with practical and concrete advice.

If criticism leaves you uncertain how to proceed, ask for more details.

If you feel uncomfortable asking your critic for more detail, or if they are unwilling to provide it, approach someone you respect or trust and ask them what they think. Do they agree with the criticism? Why or why not? Assuming this person is honest and knowledgeable, you should be able to get the answers that you need to move forward.

THANK THE CRITIC

Whether the criticism you receive is genuine or downright rude, make a point of saying "Thank you." Thanking even your harshest critics can create a lasting impression, keep you humble, and open the door to additional feedback in the future. Expressing gratitude will also make you feel better about the experience and help you alleviate any innate avoidance of feedback and criticism you may have. If you have followed these guidelines and recognize the true value of the criticism you have received, saying "Thank you" shouldn't be too difficult.

If you respect the person and their opinion, go one step further and develop a long-term mentoring relationship with them. Much like in the old days of craftsman and apprentice, a relationship with an individual whose opinion you value can go a long way in developing your skills and abilities. If nothing else, a mentor can keep you accountable to your work and help you continually improve.

*Andrew Follett is a small-business marketing director and founder of Concept Feedback (*www.conceptfeedback.com/*), a community of designers and marketers dedicated to sharing ideas and feedback on design projects.*

15

HOW TO PERSUADE YOUR USERS, BOSS, OR CLIENTS

by Paul Boag

WHETHER YOU ARE getting a client to sign off on a website's design or persuading a user to complete a call to action, we all need to know how to be convincing. Like many in the Web design industry, I have a strange job. I am part salesperson, part consultant, and part user experience designer. One day I could be pitching a new idea to a board of directors, the next I might be designing an e-commerce purchasing process. There is, however, a common theme: I spend most of my time persuading people.

120

As Web designers, we often have to nudge people in the direction we want them to go. It is a vital skill we all have to learn. We're not talking about manipulation. Underhanded techniques, and certainly lying, won't get you anywhere. But you can present yourself and your arguments in ways that make people more receptive. The first and probably most important way is to *empathize*.

The worst thing you can do is enter a meeting or begin designing a user interface with a personal agenda. If your goal is to push the other party into agreeing with you, you will meet resistance. But if you seek to understand their needs and respond to them, you will find others more cooperative.

START BY LISTENING

To achieve this, you must really listen. Paying lip service to the "idea" of listening is not enough. You have to hear what they are actually saying and look for those "points of pain" that your ideas might actually relieve:

- *Tailor presentation of the agenda:* Rather than forcing the people in the room to reluctantly agree, tailor your presentation of ideas so that they see the benefit of them. This involves some creative thinking on your part but is possible if you really understand their needs.

- *Show benefit to the other party:* Remember, explaining how your ideas will help you or others is not enough. You have to demonstrate how they help the actual people you are speaking to. For example, rather than saying to your client, "Users are going to love this new feature," you could instead say, "This new feature will keep users coming back, which will dramatically improve the number of leads you receive." Once you understand the other party and have thought about their needs, your next step is to form a relationship with them.

BE PERSONABLE

If you have a good relationship with your users, boss, or client, they will be more inclined to take your suggestions. Of course, the kind of relationship you build depends on who the other person is. Your relationship with website users is different from your relationship with your boss. However, certain approaches hold true across the board:

- *Get them nodding:* It's a silly little thing, but when I give a pitch, I try to get people to nod. Nodding is a good sign and puts people in a positive mood. I normally achieve this by repeating back to them (in different words) one of their own points. They will obviously agree with what you're saying, but it also demonstrates that you're listening and are on the same wave length.

  The same approach can be used online. For example, if I am writing a post aimed at Web designers, I know that berating IE6 will get them nodding in agreement right away. I have succeeded in making a connection.

- *Be enthusiastic:* Enthusiasm is so important. Clients want to know you care about their project. Bosses want to know you are motivated to work, and users want to know you care about the service you deliver. However, so many people lack enthusiasm when communicating their message. They come across either as defeated before they even begin or as overly aggressive. Instead, try overwhelming enthusiasm. It is infectious, and people get caught up in it. More importantly, saying "No" to somebody who is oozing enthusiasm and excitement from every pore is not easy. It would be like kicking a puppy. (Well, not quite.)

- *Mirror them:* You have probably heard how mirroring a person's body language helps establish a positive connection. Whatever you do, do not do it! Consciously doing it just comes across as creepy! It will happen naturally, so don't worry about it. That said, it is a useful indication of whether a face-to-face meeting is going well. If the other person is mirroring your body language, chances are they like you. What you can consciously do is mirror their *language* or use the same terminology.

  If your boss or client talks about "return on investment" or "success criteria," do it yourself. And if you suspect the other party is not familiar with certain terminology, make sure to avoid it. Our way of speaking associates us with a certain "tribe." If we share the same language, we are more likely to build rapport.

- *Make them smile:* Another trick for building relationships is to inject humor into the proceedings. If you can make the other person smile, you've gone a long way to breaking down any barriers. Of course, this has to be done with care. Overdo it and you'll look like the fool. But even the most miserable-looking directors on a board are human beings, too, and like to smile.

Although all of these approaches are great for building relationship, one trumps them all: openness.

BE OPEN

You may be reading this thinking, "This guy is mad. What if his clients read this stuff. Won't they feel manipulated?" My answer is no. I am open and honest about what I do. I would be entirely fine with any one of my clients reading this because nothing manipulative or secret is here. People hate being deceived, so if anything, the honesty in this article will build my relationship, not undermine it. Two key components help build open relationships and create a receptive audience:

- *Disarming honesty:* Many times, the best way to diffuse a potential conflict is with disarming honesty. For example, I regularly acknowledge in sales situations that I am there to sell and that they should take anything I say with a grain of salt. The client obviously knows this already. But verbalizing it shows a kind of honesty that people rarely encounter.

- *Be willing to show weakness:* We can sometimes be so desperate to make a point that we become unwilling to admit even the slightest weakness in our argument. Ultimately, though, we come across as pig-headed and inflexible.

People respond well when you admit you are wrong or are unsure of an answer. Be willing to say "I don't know" or "I've messed up" if necessary. People will respect you for it. One of the best examples of this is Flickr's blog post "Sometimes We Suck," in which Flickr apologizes for performance problems. By taking this approach, it demonstrated its integrity and completely defused the anger of those who were complaining. Of course, being willing to show weakness takes a lot of confidence, and that trait is critical if you are to convince others.

BE CONFIDENT

As humans we are drawn to confident leaders. We follow those who have a clear vision and walk the path with confidence. Communicating your message with confidence, therefore, is important. Establish yourself as an expert, and speak with authority.

- *Be confident, not arrogant:* Being confident also means having the strength to admit when you are wrong. A truly confident leader does not claim to have all of the answers all of the time. Being able to concede points and allow others to express their views is a key aspect of confidence. Only those who lack confidence fear opposing views.

- *You do not always have to win:* Pick your battles. Conceding some points to achieve the greater aim is okay. Giving ground does not undermine your position. Sometimes you have to be a little submissive to get people on board. Don't allow your ego to get in the way. If someone feels good about having won an argument, they will more likely be accommodating when you suggest an alternative. Compromising sometimes is okay. It is certainly better than constantly being negative and rejecting counter-proposals.

BE POSITIVE

Whether dealing with a demanding boss, difficult client, or finicky users, you have to impress them with your attitude and service. Always be helpful and keen to leave a positive impression. In customer service, that sometimes involves going the extra mile. With your boss, it means seeing the benefits of their latest mad scheme. Whatever the situation, developing a reputation for being unhelpful and negative is the worst thing that can happen.

123

CONCLUSION

There are no Jedi mind tricks that will help you to always convince your clients that you are right. At the end of the day, the secret to persuading others is to show respect, listen to their opinions, and present your vision in language that they understand.

Paul Boag is the founder of the UK Web design agency Headscape, author of the Website Owners Manual, *and host of the award-winning Web design podcast Boagworld.*

16

HOW TO CREATE THE PERFECT CLIENT QUESTIONNAIRE

by Cameron Chapman

DISCOVERING WHAT YOUR clients really want is one of the most fundamental steps in creating a good working relationship. If you can figure out exactly what your clients want for their website up front, it will save both of you time and frustration later.

Creating a client questionnaire isn't complicated, though it can be a bit time-consuming if you don't know where to start. You have to think about who your clients are and what information you need from them, and then go from there. Following is a complete guide to creating a custom questionnaire for your design business.

WHY YOU NEED A QUESTIONNAIRE

A client questionnaire serves two purposes. The first is to figure out what the new website should achieve. The second is to figure out what the client wants the website to look like.

Both of these things are very important to find out up front. By figuring out what your client wants and needs, you can avoid delivering something to them that doesn't fit the direction in which they want to take their website.

Without a good client questionnaire, you could end up having to go back to your client repeatedly throughout the project to get more information or clarification on what they really want. You could also waste a lot time designing and coding things that aren't quite what the client is looking for. A good questionnaire removes a lot of the guesswork in designing and makes it a better experience for both parties.

FORMULATING YOUR QUESTIONS

Your questions should get to the root of your client's needs. They should also help you assess your client's likes and dislikes.

Take the time to customize your questionnaire with the information that you most often need from clients. The types of websites you usually design, the industries you work with most, and the level of technical knowledge your clients tend to have can all determine the kinds of questions you will include and how they are phrased.

BACKGROUND AND GENERAL QUESTIONS

Before you dive into the questions that will suss out how your client wants their website to look and what they want it to do, you need to get an idea of what the client is all about and why they're looking for a new website. This section of your questionnaire can be very revealing, especially if they're unhappy with their current website.

You'll also want to get some general information in this section. Ask about the budget for the project, who you'll be working with directly, who the decision-makers are, and what staff are going to be involved in the design process and what their roles will be. Find out who their target visitor is, who their customers are, how they're currently interacting with those customers online, and how they'd like to improve that interaction. And make sure to find out whether they already have a domain name and hosting package that they're happy with.

Here are some sample questions to gather background and general information:

> Why are you looking for a new website design or redesign?
>
> What do you like most about your current website?
>
> What do you dislike most about your current website?
>
> Do you already have a domain name and hosting plan?

FUNCTION-FOCUSED QUESTIONS

Figuring out what exactly your client wants their website to do is key to making sure you give them what they want. You need to ask them questions that strike at the heart of exactly what they want from their website. Sounds easy enough, right? Except in many cases, clients don't really know what they want their website to do. Your questionnaire can actually help them clarify their needs and wants.

Some example questions for figuring out how the website should function:

Do you want to sell products on your website?

Do you want a contact form or any other forms on your website?

Do you need an image gallery, video, or other multimedia content?

Do you want a blog or other regularly updated content?

DESIGN-FOCUSED QUESTIONS

Finally, you'll want some information about the aesthetics of your client. Now, in an ideal world, your client will have perused your portfolio and seen the kinds of websites you design and will have decided to work with you because they like your aesthetic. But that's not always the case. Figuring out their design preferences up front helps you avoid designing something they will hate later on.

You have a few different ways to learn their tastes. Ask your client what colors they'd like to use. They may have a set color scheme or have colors associated with their brand. Or they may be open to your input. The same could be done for qualities that they want their website to be associated with (e.g., "bold," "soft," "professional," "informal," etc.).

One of the best ways to get a sense of your client's design preferences is to ask them to provide you with examples of a few websites that have designs they like and a few websites whose designs they don't like. Also ask them what they like or dislike about each of these designs, because this sheds light on their overall tastes.

Another, sometimes more telling, method of doing this is to show them five to ten websites and ask them what they like and dislike about each. This is often more effective, because you can choose websites that have a wide range of styles and get a fuller picture of what they like and don't like.

Here are some sample questions to figure out the client's design tastes:

Do you have a color scheme you'd like to use?

What words would you like people to associate with your website?

Do you have a specific style of design in mind?

WHAT NOT TO ASK

I don't know how many times I've seen questionnaires ask things that are either completely irrelevant or too technical for the average client to understand. Remember that your clients likely don't know much about the technical aspects of design. They probably know they want something like an image gallery or a map, but they won't know whether the things they want will require a custom database or JavaScript. In many cases, they might not even know basics, like whether their website should have an RSS feed or Flash.

Here are some examples of unhelpful questions:

Will you need a custom database?

Will you need JavaScript (jQuery, MooTools, etc.)?

Will you need an e-commerce solution?

Will you need to handle uploading and downloading?

Will you need a searchable database?

While getting an idea of what the technical specifications of the website might be is important, structure your questions around the features and benefits of the website, not the specifications. So instead of the preceding questions, ask things like:

Would you like a search engine on your website?

Should visitors be able to download files from your website or post their own files?

Would you like visitors to be able to sign up for accounts, or would you like a secure area just for visitors who have signed up for accounts?

Would you like to sell products on your website?

PLANNING FOR THE FUTURE

Make sure to ask clients about their future needs, too. If you know they might want an e-commerce solution six months down the road, make provisions for that in the initial website design. The goal is to build a long-term relationship with the client, so the more involved you are in their goals and plans, the easier your job will be now and in the future.

You'll also want to ask clients about regular updates and maintenance for the website. And you'll want an idea of how much updating and maintaining they will want to handle in-house and how much they might want you to do. Some sample questions:

> How often do you want or will you need to make updates to your website?
>
> Do you have someone in your company who will be responsible for ongoing website updates?
>
> Does that person have any experience with website maintenance?
>
> What features do you anticipate adding to your website in the future?

TIPS TO REFINE YOUR QUESTIONNAIRE

Once you have a basic questionnaire mapped out, it's time to make some refinements so that you get the best results from it. The goal of the questionnaire is to improve your workflow and communication, so you want the process to be as efficient and effective as possible.

First, keep the questionnaire short. You want as much information from your clients as possible, but if your questionnaire is too long, your clients will get bored and may not give it the attention it deserves.

There are two ways to keep the questionnaire short: limit the number of questions and/or limit the length of questions. Refine your questions until they are as short as possible (five to ten words is plenty).

Don't be afraid to be creative with some questions to get your clients thinking outside the box. Ask a few unorthodox questions. Ask them to compare their website to something unrelated (such as a building or a food). You could provide sample answers to guide your clients to giving you the information you're looking for.

Continue to refine your questionnaire over time and as you get client feedback. Consider adapting the questionnaire to individual clients to get information that is more relevant to particular projects. It's your questionnaire: use it the way that works best for you and your clients.

Cameron Chapman is a professional web and graphic designer with over six years of experience. She writes for a number of blogs, including her own, Cameron Chapman On Writing. *She's also the author of* Internet Famous: A Practical Guide to Becoming an Online Celebrity.

III

MARKETING: EFFECTIVE STRATEGIES FOR FREELANCERS

17

GETTING CLIENTS: APPROACHING THE COMPANY

by Peter Smart

A DEFINING FACTOR in any freelancer or agency's success in gaining new business is their ability to market their skills effectively. In this chapter, we explore ways in which designers can strategically promote themselves to get new clients. Securing new business by approaching companies can be a very challenging process, full of pitfalls. Here, we look at a couple of steps that will help you impress potential clients and avoid the most common mistakes.

STEP ONE: BE FOCUSED

A focused approach to work is paramount for success. Freelancers often take on every job opportunity that presents itself. Although this would rapidly expand your showcase of work, more often than not it leaves you over-stretched, with a portfolio of odds and ends instead of specialized results. Focus instead on who you would like to work with. This could be based on several factors, such as:

- *Industry.* By specializing in a particular industry, such as health care or retail, you build a portfolio of relevant experience. Although this could limit your workload initially, you will be actively working toward identifying yourself as someone with expertise in your chosen field.

- *Media.* Deciding which media and platforms to specialize in is important for any firm or individual. For many, the choice is between specializing in print and digital communication. This distinction will, again, allow you to focus and build relevant knowledge that you can then offer to your clients.

- *Geographical location.* You may also wish to focus your efforts on a particular geographical location. This could be a neighborhood, city, or region. With this approach, your advertising in local media can be more personal and targeted, and you ensure easy traveling between you and clients.

STEP TWO: BE INSIGHTFUL

Once you have established the kind of organizations you would like to work with, learn how their businesses work. Visit a range of websites in the field and ask yourself some key questions, such as:

- *Who do they work with?* Knowing who your clients work with will give you an indication of how you can be of service to them. For example, an insurance firm looking to target university students might need to refresh its flyer and leaflet campaign in time for the beginning of term.

- *What are the company's ethics?* Most established organizations put a vision statement on their website. This will give you key insight into a company's values, history, growth, and future direction. This information is invaluable because it will help you better understand how the business operates and, thus, how you can tailor your approach to it. For example, if the company has a progressive stance on sustainability and the environment, you could approach them with ideas for paperless advertising and communication.

- *Does it have an advertising budget?* Although this will not be explicitly stated, by reviewing a business' prior advertising you will be able to estimate how much capital it typically invests in design per annum. Again, this allows you to tailor your marketing proposal to its budget.

These kinds of questions will give you important insight into the services that an organization requires and, therefore, what services you can offer.

STEP THREE: BE PERSONAL

The power of face-to-face contact should not be underestimated. A common temptation for graphic designers is to manage their small empire from behind a desk over the Internet. Although work can be found online, the relationship between client and designer is often fleeting.

Build strong links with your clients, which will increase the likelihood of repeat business. One of the most important skills to learn, then, is face-to-face meetings. Meeting a client face to face forces them to give you their undivided attention. You will be able to convey your passion much more effectively and personally.

Actively seek out opportunities to meet potential clients face to face. Cold-calling or emailing can be a tiring and disheartening experience and may give you limited results. Instead, when approaching a business for the first time, find out the name and contact details of the marketing director, which you can often find on the company's website. If it's not there, make a quick phone call to ask for it.

Before making your first contact with a client, do your research. Familiarize yourself with their business and understand what they do. When you're ready to make contact, have a few short sentences prepared that summarize the specific information you wish to communicate. This should include your:

- *Introduction.* Explain who you are and why you are calling. Although this may seem obvious, establishing these facts is crucial to presenting yourself clearly and memorably. This could be as simple as: "Good afternoon. My name is Peter Smart, and I am calling on behalf of Roam Design."
- *Hook or pitch.* Once you have established who you are, engage your potential client. Mentioning that you specialize in their particular industry and that you offer a range of tailored services is an attractive proposition and good way to begin. Alternatively, you could begin with a hook. A hook is a one-off special offer that makes your services more attractive. This could be offering 50 percent off the cost of design work in November or a free hour of consultation.
- *Call to action.* Establish the next step your client should take. Offer to meet them and consult in person, at a time and location suitable to them.

STEP FOUR: BE PREPARED

Once you have arranged your meeting, research the company more extensively. Make notes on key areas of interest to develop later. For example, you could look at the company's:

- *Advertising.* The company's media presence is a good indication of its capacities in communication. Look at where it advertises, how it does it, and where it doesn't advertise. If it does not advertise online, you could present this as a possibility.

- *Branding.* If possible, source a variety of the company's marketing material. Examine it and note anything you would do differently.
- *Website.* Does the company have a website? If not, this could be a great opportunity to expand its online presence. If it does, look at the structure, content, and presentation. Note areas for improvement and, more importantly, why they could be improved.

Having an informed opinion on the strengths and weaknesses of the company's current marketing and perceived identity allow you to guide it to services that would benefit it. You may also find it helpful to compare its advertising to that of its competitors.

Also, prepare your "elevator pitch," which is a brief summary of your business, its aims and how it helps clients. Being able to explain what you do concisely demonstrates that your business goals are clear and your approach targeted.

STEP FIVE: BE UNIQUE

Standing out from the crowd is difficult, especially if you are an emerging talent. To stand out, come up with original ideas on how the company can market itself. Suggest options it may not yet have considered, such as viral marketing, Web-based promotion, or targeted leafleting, and demonstrate how they would improve business.

Impress the client and exceed his expectations. If you are going to propose a website redesign, take time before your meeting to produce a few drafts of what it could look like. You could present alongside a concise wireframe showing how the information could be better presented. Alternatively, if you will be proposing to refresh the company's branding and identity, bring some visual stimuli to support your argument. Don't present a whole new identity, but rather suggest colors, layouts, typefaces, and advertising formats that could guide the conversation.

The client will want evidence of your skill to deliver on your ideas, so bring your portfolio along to impress them, along with references and endorsements from previous clients.

STEP SIX: BE PROFESSIONAL

Your first meeting with the potential client is of paramount importance because it will determine whether you gain their business. To make a good impression, be meticulous in your preparation. Research and plan your presentation well so that you are confident in your delivery and can support your proposals with facts. This means you should have a firm grasp of the figures and costs associated with your proposal.

For example, if you will be proposing an inner-city billboard and bus-stop marketing campaign, know the costs involved in producing large-format printing and renting advertising space. Find out the number of people who will see the advertisements daily. This will give the client a balanced appreciation of both the outlay and the benefits of your proposal.

Equally important is your appearance. Invest in a suit or smart business-wear. This will impress upon them that you are serious about what you do, which will make them take you seriously, too.

STEP SEVEN: BE ATTENTIVE

Listen to the client. This step is often missed by designers who are overly keen to explain their innovative ideas. Listening is a powerful tool. It shows you truly care about what the client has to say. Take notes on any information they offer about the company, its plans, and immediate requirements.

STEP EIGHT: BE RESOURCEFUL

Every meeting with a client is an opportunity and should not be taken lightly. Approach meetings resourcefully and demonstrate your professionalism. You could even prepare a package of materials to leave with them, including:

- *Business card.* Always have a business card on hand. It should have your name, contact details and, ideally, a website where they can see samples of your work.
- *Samples of work.* You might also want to leave a mini-printed portfolio of some of your best and most relevant work. Even if you don't win that particular project, your details and experience will be in their file for future reference.
- *Curriculum Vitae.* A CV is a useful record of relevant work experience and is a good place to list your previous clients and technical competencies.

Remember, the decision about which freelancer to hire may not rest with one person in the organization. By adhering to this simple step, you allow others who are involved in the process to see your work at their convenience, making your application even stronger.

STEP NINE: BE COMMITTED

If you do not hear from the client immediately, don't panic or give up hope. Wait a few days, and then send a polite email, thanking them for their time. In the email, reiterate in brief your proposal and mention how you would love to work with them. Then wait. If you receive no response within three weeks of your meeting, you may want to re-inquire by telephone. Chances are, they have not forgotten about you; moreover, your call will demonstrate your enthusiasm and commitment.

STEP TEN: EVALUATE

Whether or not your meeting was successful, you can learn something from it. Evaluate your performance, what you did well and, importantly, what you could improve. Learn from your mistakes, and rectify them for your next venture. Your ability to do this plays a vital role in your future success.

CONCLUSION

These are just ten of the key steps to consider when approaching a company. Remember: be bold, be proactive, and don't be afraid to make mistakes. Every person has their own methods of finding work, but learning these steps could be the difference between realizing a dream and settling for second best.

Starting his company at the age of 15, Peter Smart runs the award-winning creative marketing consultancy Roam Design. With an impressive portfolio, Roam Design creates cutting-edge brand experiences for domestic and international clients.

18

CONVERTING PROSPECTS INTO CLIENTS

by Alyssa Gregory

THE ABILITY TO communicate, and communicate well, is one of the biggest factors in business success. You could be an excellent designer, but if you're unable to promote your services and communicate effectively with clients and colleagues, your potential is limited. The principal areas where communication is essential include:

- Pitching potential clients
- Client meetings
- Customer service
- Face-to-face networking
- Marketing your business

PITCHING POTENTIAL CLIENTS

When you freelance or own a business, your livelihood depends on your ability to sell your services. You need to be able to convince prospects that you are the best person for the job, and the communication secrets in this article will help you do this successfully.

ASK THE RIGHT QUESTIONS

Part of selling your services is being able to understand the client's unique needs. You can do this only by asking questions that get to the heart of the challenges they are facing. Once you have a clear understanding of the problem that the client needs to solve, you can pitch your services as the best possible option for the client, outlining how you will meet their needs.

For example, when I am contacted by a prospective client, I have them fill out a website requirements document that poses various questions to help me better understand what they are looking for in a website. Some of the questions I ask are:

- Describe the nature of your business.
- Who is your target audience?
- What is the background on the project? (Is it brand new? Has it already begun?)
- What are the goals and objectives of the project?
- What is the timeline for the project?

COMMUNICATE PROFESSIONALLY

Your professionalism can win you contracts, and your communication skills add to the complete package. Take time to proofread all emails prior to sending; use a business email address with a proper signature; answer the phone professionally; and speak articulately and competently at all times.

While my email signature has evolved over time, below is the general format I follow, which has worked well for me:

> Name
> Company | Website
> Email | Phone number

CLIENT MEETINGS

Client meetings, even those that take place over the telephone, are an integral part of every successful business. Follow these tips to make your meetings as productive as possible.

SCHEDULE AND PREPARE THOROUGHLY

We're all busy these days, so scheduling your meetings in advance ensures that you and your clients have an adequate amount of uninterrupted time to speak. Once your meeting is scheduled, take time to prepare an agenda that outlines focus points and sets a structure. Sharing the agenda for the meeting gives both you and the client an opportunity to fully prepare.

Because you may not be using the same calendar or scheduling program as your client, confirming the date and time of your meetings in an email and sending a reminder and the agenda the day before is good practice. If you are unsure how to format an agenda, plenty of templates are available for free online.

SPEAK, PAUSE, LISTEN

When you have several topics to tackle, rushing through them to get all of your ideas out may be tempting. But this causes confusion and makes the client feel that their input is not important. Slow down, and remember that communication is a two-way street. Establish a give-and-take that allows both parties to have their say.

One way to become a better listener is to limit or eliminate distractions during your conversations. That may mean closing your email client, turning off the television, and closing the door to your office. By doing these small things, you ensure that the client has your full attention, and they will sense that, too.

FOLLOW UP IN WRITING

While you may be taking notes during phone or in-person meetings, the other party might not be, so follow up after the meeting with a written message, giving an overview of the discussion to make sure you are both on the same page. Summarize what was agreed, repeat questions that were raised and outline the next steps and responsibilities for both parties. In addition to sending your notes, invite the other party to give their feedback on what you have sent. This way, it becomes a collaborative document and not just one person's view.

CUSTOMER SERVICE

Your clients want to feel that they are your priority. You can make them feel so by providing exemplary customer service. Try these communication-focused actions to improve your customer service.

ASK FOR FEEDBACK

One way to maintain long-term relationships with your clients is by keeping open lines of communication. This means asking them for their input on how things are going and how they feel about the service you're providing. This can be accomplished by inquiring at the end of a project, during day-to-day conversations, or through formal surveys. The format matters less than the actual act of it, so work it into your business and fine tune as you go along.

When conducting surveys, use an online service that tracks responses for you. There are several online services that should give you enough functionality to conduct client surveys.

ADDRESS PROBLEMS

If a client is unhappy, don't ignore their complaints. Ask them why they are unhappy and what you can do to fix the situation. The longer you wait to bring it up, the worse it will get. Addressing the issue and being accountable when appropriate puts you on the path to resolution. And your willingness to face the problem head-on tells the client that you care about the project and their satisfaction.

If a client complains about your turnaround time or responsiveness, you may need to create a more formal project plan to clarify expectations. A working document like this can also eliminate some of the uncertainty regarding responsibilities and keep everyone on track.

TRY A NEW FORMAT

If a problem with your client stems from miscommunication, try a different method of communication. If you have been handling everything via email, schedule a phone call to see if that clears things up.

After the call, you can summarize the conversation in an email to the client, which will give you another opportunity to get both of you on the same page again.

Today, so much communication is done via email that the opportunity for major miscommunication is almost inevitable. A rule of thumb is to limit your email to one screen-full (i.e., above the fold); anything that requires more space than that should be handled by phone. This should help you avoid some of the pitfalls of relying on email alone.

FACE-TO-FACE NETWORKING

Networking events, conferences, and other face-to-face opportunities can take your business to a new level. These tips focus on helping you get the most from in-person networking activities.

COMMUNICATE CONFIDENTLY

Be confident and use body language to support that confidence. Shake hands firmly, smile, and make eye contact while communicating at live networking events. Don't forget to bring business cards to hand out to everyone you meet, and remember to relax and be yourself.

Before heading out to a networking event, practice introducing yourself to new people to gain confidence. Working on your introduction with someone you trust and asking for their feedback also helps.

PREPARE AN ELEVATOR SPEECH

An elevator speech helps you make the most of a first impression, while making networking situations easier and more productive. Be prepared with your speech and ready to answer common questions about your business and what you do. Practice your elevator speech ahead of time so that you are relaxed and comfortable with introducing yourself.

Your elevator speech should last no longer than 30 seconds and should convey how your product or service solves a problem for your target audience. An elevator speech could go something like:

> *Have you ever gotten completely lost on a website because the navigation was inconsistent, confusing, and disorganized? What I do is redesign websites for small-business owners who need a stronger, more coherent online presence. By learning as much as I can about the company, I create a strategic plan for reinventing an existing website to be more functional and user-friendly.*

MARKETING YOUR SERVICES

Whether you market your business online, in person, or through traditional advertising, communication is key to brand awareness. Here are two secrets to magnify the impact of your marketing across the board.

BE RESPONSIVE

A big part of marketing is being available to your target audience and following up when necessary. If you market your business through social media outlets — including Twitter, Facebook, and blogging — watch for and respond to comments, questions, and especially complaints. And when you are contacted as a result of offline marketing activities, respond quickly and professionally.

Plenty of recent examples on Twitter show how certain brands have been slow to respond to criticism, hoping it would die down, only to see it spin out of control. Also, when you do respond on social media websites, keep it professional, and avoid confrontation because that will only spread the fire.

WRITE WELL

You can't successfully promote your business if your marketing copy is not clear, concise, and action-provoking. If writing is not your forte, consider hiring someone to help you craft copy that attracts potential clients, generates interest in your services, and motivates potential clients to action.

To strengthen your writing skills, start a swipe file of marketing copy that you like and have found inspirational. Read through it and make notes of what you like in particular and what pulls you in. By making this a frequent exercise, you should be able to learn what makes good copy good and bad copy bad.

147

YOUR TURN TO WEIGH IN

The difference between being a tolerable communicator and a truly effective communicator is the difference between being good and great at what you do. If your design skills are up to par with your competition's, then strong communication skills can put you ahead. Strengthening your communication skills is worth the time and effort, and you may be surprised by how much you benefit from more polished and professional interaction.

Alyssa Gregory is the owner of avertua, LLC, a full-service virtual assistant firm. She has a passion for supporting small businesses, and provides business tips, advice, and news through her business blog, the Small Business Idea Generator.

19

MARKETING RULES AND PRINCIPLES FOR FREELANCERS

by Jeff Gardner

FREELANCERS HAVE IT hard. I mean, really hard. In theory, the idea of working for yourself, of being able to choose who you work with and what you work on, sounds like the perfect job. In practice though, it's a lot more than just working on amazing projects for amazing clients from the comfort of your own home.

There is a tremendous amount of competition out there, and a lot of it is willing to play dirty, cut-throat, and underhanded to beat you to the clients. How are you supposed to get ahead of those guys? Is it even possible to earn an honest buck? Thankfully, it is possible and can be a lot easier than you think.

MARKETING IS A BRAND GAME

Marketing and its in-your-face division advertising are all about one thing: building brand equity. If you take away only one concept from this article, please let it be this one! In this Internet-fueled economy, brand strength is everything! But brand and brand equity are often misunderstood concepts. The easiest way to think about brand equity is that it's the sum total of feelings people get when they think about your business or service. And it's important to remember that brand equity can be positive or negative.

A company like Kiva (www.kiva.org/) has copious amounts of positive brand equity — their business impacts the world in a positive way and they are nearly universally liked because they are fair and pleasant to work with.

On the other hand, negative brand equity (like Mr. Madoff), is that horrible, sinking feeling that people get whenever your name is mentioned, which, as you can imagine, makes doing business very difficult.

Brand equity is one of the most monumentally important parts of running a successful business. If people associate your business with nice feelings and positive images, they will want to work with you. If they associate nothing but letdowns and suffering with your brand, it doesn't matter how good your work is, no one will ever come knocking.

LET'S TAKE IT FROM THE TOP

From the very first step setting out as a freelancer, you're giving up the security of a consistent paycheck for the freedom to work with who you want and when you want. There are a lot of risks, but there are also plenty of rewards for those who succeed. First time freelancers and those just starting out often ask about how to find those initial clients. A reasonable request: but one that is, unfortunately, very hard to answer. Starting a business, especially a one-man shop (the way that most freelancers operate) is a very individual process. Everyone has their own story and their own path. However, after conversations with many freelancers and my own experiences, I've learned that there are a few common themes that can go a long way toward helping rookie freelancers get up and running.

IT PAYS TO HAVE A PLAN

In the beginning, it's tempting to try and take every job that comes your way. But taking every job is a mistake. You will end up overstretched on vastly different projects, trying to work with clients in industries that you know nothing about. Instead, take some time before you even start trying to recruit clients to formulate a plan. Ask yourself what type of work you want to do, with what types of clients? Knowing your audience and knowing your focus from the outset will help you to qualify prospects and qualify their projects.

For example, imagine that, after much reflection and research, you decide that you want to focus solely on designing and building web pages for Broadway actors. You live in New York City and many of your friends are actors, plus you just love the theatre. From that decision, you now have a clearly defined market and a clearly defined product for that market. Finding prospects and explaining your business becomes easier for you, and easier for those prospects to understand.

THE ELEVATOR PITCH

An elevator pitch is a one and a half to two minute summation of what your business is and how it benefits your prospective clients. If you can't concisely explain what it is that you do and how it helps your clients in that short amount of time, it's a pretty good indication that you need to focus your business goals a little more.

Having a clearly defined plan also simplifies the process of qualifying clients and potential projects: If it doesn't fit into your plan, don't take the work. It's that simple. It may feel counter-productive at the start to be turning prospective clients away but, remember, you're in this for the long haul and building a brand around your work takes time, commitment, and focus. You can't build a brand by working for everyone, doing whatever project they happen to have.

EVERY PERSON YOU KNOW IS YOUR AUDIENCE

When you're constructing your plan, it's important to think about what you want to work on and where you want to be in the future, but don't forget to include the groups that you are already a part of and the people you already know. Your hobbies can be a great source of business and a great way to get your freelancing business off the ground. If you have a lot of friends that are actors, and you love the theatre, that might be a good industry to focus on.

If you really love photography, you can focus on serving galleries or photographers. If you already know you're passionate about the subject material, doing the work becomes that much easier! And you've already won half the battle with the people that know (and trust) you, so don't be afraid to ask. Family, friends, former co-workers; they are all potential clients. A word of warning though; mixing business with pleasure can be dangerous territory and certainly not the area for hard selling tactics. Here are a few guidelines to make sure your sales pitch remains respectful of your current relationships:

- *Make sure you're clear about your intentions.* If you're starting a new business, it should be clear that you are going to be charging for your services. Be certain, from the start, that your potential client (and friend) knows that you're not giving work away for free.
- *Only offer help where you can make an honest, positive difference.* These people trust you; don't abuse that trust just to build your portfolio. In the long run, your friendship (and your reputation) is more important than your portfolio.

- *Start small and over-deliver.* Don't promise the moon in order to sell your services. It's always better to start with a small project and execute it perfectly. If you have an idea on how to expand the project, discuss it after you've proven you're a genius.

BUY LOCAL, BE LOCAL

Another good place to start is by focusing locally. While it's certainly more intimidating to walk into a local business and try to sell your services face to face, it can also be a lot more powerful. It is important to remember that not everyone is as comfortable with doing business over the Internet as us web professionals; for many clients, it's easier to put trust in another local business because they can see and touch the person with whom they are doing business. Physical meetings settle fears about fly-by-night Internet operations that might just be trying to get their check and deliver something sub-standard.

But face-to-face selling is a lot more difficult than sending out a few hundred emails and waiting for the responses to come pouring in. Here are a few tips for successful face-to-face selling:

- *Be prepared.* It's not just for the Boy Scouts! Make sure you understand your client's business before you walk through the door. It's an instant credibility booster when you can show that you clearly understand the problems that your prospective client is facing.

- *Show your past successes.* Have a few anecdotes and a few samples of your work ready to show. Not an entire tome of every site you've ever had a hand in — just a few of the best will suffice.

- *Don't be afraid to ask.* When you've shown that you understand your prospective client's issues and challenges and you've established the quality of your work, it's time to ask for what you want. Don't beat around the bush, just tell the prospective client what benefit you can provide them and how much it will cost them. Be forthcoming and honest about what you charge and, above all, don't be embarrassed about the number you give them; this is business, after all.

Working locally is also a great way to build a community around your brand. A community that you can touch and feel and talk to on a regular basis can be a gold mine for freelancers because smaller, local-run businesses are generally well connected with each other and are quick to offer recommendations (when deserved) to other local businesses.

I've heard of freelancers that have built websites for, quite literally, every small- to medium-sized business in their town. They started with one and, based on glowing recommendations and personal connections, were comfortably in work for years to come.

EXPANDING YOUR REACH

So you've established yourself, you've got a steady flow of business and you're relatively comfortable, but how do you take your business to the next level? How can you earn more while maintaining the same hours?

Hitting an earnings plateau is a common problem for small businesses, especially one-person operations. Sure, you could bring in employees or subcontract out some of your work to other freelancers but your underlying problem still remains. You are doing work for other small- to medium-sized businesses that can only afford to pay a certain amount. To make the jump into a higher tax bracket, the name of the game is brand recognition and differentiation. People far and wide need to know your brand and they need to have an acute understanding of why they know your brand. In essence, you need to set your business apart from, and above, the competition.

CAST A WIDE NET

Moving from a client base of small fish to one of big fish takes time and, unless you live in one of the major corporate centers of the world, it takes geographical expansion. You cannot source all of your work locally anymore — and this is where advertising comes into play.

Contrary to what many web personalities these days would have you believe, advertising is not dead. No, in fact, it's more alive and more helpful than you may know! The trick with advertising though, is getting it right:

- *Favor highly targeted, captive audiences.* Place your ads within ad networks that cater only to your design/development niche. Broad campaigns are costly and yield low conversion rates, whereas targeted ads to people who are actively looking for a web designer or developer can cost far less and provide many more conversions.

- *Place the ads yourself.* By directly contacting small niche blogs and other sites that you know to be frequented by the exact clients you hope to attract you can generally pay less for advertising space. In addition, forming a relationship with the people on the other end is likely to allow you more control over when and how your ads are shown.

- *Maintain a consistent message.* Make sure that all of your advertising is consistent with your brand. And I'm not just talking about the design of your ads. Your message and your tone are just as important as how your ad looks. Consistency across all of these areas will help to build a solid brand identity.
- *Publicity Stunts 2.0.* Better yet, save those ad dollars, challenge yourself to pull off something incredible in a short period of time (build a working web app in 12 hours, etc.) or redesign the homepage of a potential client's site and then send them the redesign idea with your sales pitch included.

It's important to note: You can't just run a few ads and expect the business to just pour in. Effective advertising takes time and, above all, constant measurement to be successful. Start small and keep good records of new business that is a direct result from your advertising efforts. This way you can focus your spending on efforts that pay off and drop advertising with little to no return on investment.

LET THE LOVE GROW

You've heard it before, but it's so important that it's worth mentioning again: Teaching the world what you know is a tremendously powerful method of establishing credibility and bringing in new clients. If you've established your business as the expert in a given niche of design or development, you've more than likely built an incredible store of very specific knowledge and experience. While it would seem to make good sense to keep that information to yourself (in order to preserve your competitive advantage) the opposite is actually true.

Write guest posts on influential blogs, post frequently to your own blog, make sure you're helping as many other designers or developers as you can. Every new place you can get your name and your information only helps to spread your brand and solidify your status as an expert. And contrary to belittling your competitive advantage (remember, competitive advantage is a multi-headed monster and it takes more than just your knowledge to take your place in the market), it fortifies your position in the market as the most knowledgeable and skilled practitioner in your field.

Need an example? Think about the chefs of high-end restaurants: Why do you think they are so happy to write cookbooks full of their most prized recipes? I'm sure the big royalty checks help, but it's because they know it takes more than the ingredient list to make a beautiful and delicious dish, and that those cookbooks are helping thousands of people cook better food for themselves, which only serves to build their positive brand equity and name recognition.

CHARGE MORE

Yup. Simple idea right? You want to earn more? Then charge more. If you have a constant stream of good business, and especially if you have to turn clients away because you are too busy, you should be charging more for your services.

Working too many hours? Raise your prices and you'll cull some of the price-conscious clients off the bottom. Chances are, you'll be earning the same or more from fewer hours. A wedding photographer that I know has been steadily raising her prices since about the third client she ever got and it's only fueled her business. She is now charging at least double what she was originally charging and continues to increase her client base.

Something to remember about price changes, though. If you are going to raise your prices, give fair warning to your current and possible future clients with an announcement on your blog about the price hike. Being honest and forthcoming about what your prices will be and why you are becoming more expensive will generally quell any opposition from clients about the higher price tag on your services.

Hopefully I've given some hope to those newbie freelancers out there and some encouragement to those sitting on the earnings plateau. And I hope that everyone has taken away the idea that, more than any other single concept, the idea of brand equity should be the paramount concern in any marketing effort you decide to follow!

Jeff Gardner is a business nerd who loves spreadsheets, graphs, and helping companies figure out how to perform better. He also enjoys writing, photography, and being outside.

20

HOW MANY IDEAS DO YOU SHOW YOUR CLIENTS?

by Graham Smith

I READ SOMEWHERE that showing your client the full range of your creative ideas during a project is important, the rationale being that the client is entitled to see the ideas coming from the creative professional who they have hired and invested in. While this approach has some benefits, in some cases showing too many ideas is counter-productive to the natural flow of a project. Proof of how imaginative you are can be shown in other ways.

SPOILED FOR CHOICE

Consider these two alternative scenarios.

SCENARIO 1

You look at your Illustrator pasteboard and see half a dozen cool logo ideas . . . not just cool, but super-cool . . . not just super-cool, actually, but practical and appropriate. You have translated the brief brilliantly. You feel rather pleased with yourself. However, the last time you showed a client all of your ideas, you got caught up in a dizzying merry-go-round, forced to mash up parts of one logo with parts of another, using unsuitable and under-baked concepts.

That client was overwhelmed with ideas and unable to choose one or the other: too many directions, and too many good ideas. You offered all your super-cool ideas on a platter, convinced that you had nailed all possible directions. You worked hard to pre-empt your client's questions and suggestions. But with all of this hard work, you unwittingly set in motion a series of events that many designers before you have experienced.

Putting your client in the position of a kid in candy store can lead to some of the more frustrating experiences in design work. Are we undermining the flow of a project with our need to have our creative ego stroked by the client?

Too much choice can be a bad thing for clients.

SCENARIO 2

Again, looking at your Illustrator pasteboard, you see half a dozen cool logo ideas: super-cool, practical and appropriate, in fact. You have translated the brief brilliantly, as before.

The client is impressed by your imagination, your interpretation of the brief, and your ability to think outside the box. They feel embarrassed — even spoiled — by the choice of amazing ideas; not what they were expecting, given their previous experiences. The client looks at the ideas and realizes you were the right person for the job. They go away to mull over the ideas.

You're pleased. The client is pleased. Time for a beer.

The client returns with a decisive plan of attack. They have picked out one or several potential winners from among your ideas and are keen to walk through tweaks and changes with you. By showing the client all of your ideas, whether cool or funky, practical or safe, you have covered all bases, left no room for misinterpretation, and accounted for that notion of "subjective perceptions."

As is almost always the case, you have your own favorites, but prior experience has shown that you mustn't assume the client will feel the same.

FEWER IDEAS, LESS CHOICE

We could alter these two scenarios by changing the "showing all ideas" to "showing just a few." The advantages would be that the client would not be overwhelmed: you will have provided just a few promising ideas. This way, you are being assertive and confident in your ability to interpret the brief. You also believe that the client would be handicapped by more choice.

In both cases, the client might be pleased with the ideas you have picked out and your ability to get the job done. You are a creative laser-guided missile. You don't need your ego stroked, and you don't need to show off your awesome imagination to every client. Your portfolio does that just fine.

You have many other cool and practical ideas up your sleeve, but putting all your cards on the table at this time is not necessary. Save them. If the client does not buy any of the ideas you've filtered for them, even after you have justified their suitability, you can fall back on those. Even if you lose round 1, you're prepared for round 2.

159

BE AWARE

Consider these points before attempting a full-360 triple-duck-tailed high-board dive. This is not a comprehensive list but a good starting point when deciding whether to show some or all of your ideas.

KNOWING YOUR CLIENT: A PSYCHOLOGICAL ANGLE

Ultimately, your flexibility in your presentation of ideas will be determined by how well you know the client: getting a good sense of their personality, their brief, and other personality- and business-related issues. You will also have to know the process that your contact will go through back at their base: are they the decider, or do they report back to a board or senior staff member?

When a group of people is involved in making decisions, you may want to keep a tighter rein on the creative process. Presenting too many ideas to one person can be overwhelming, but too many ideas for a board of six spells disaster.

Being able to read people is not only useful: it can save your sanity over time. Design and creativity are one thing, but if you want to excel at business and attract new clients, especially as a freelancer, being well versed in basic psychology goes a long way.

COVER YOUR BACK: A SOLID BRIEF

A well-prepared brief is always essential and one of the first things to cover before doing anything creative. Research the company. Understand its decision-making structure. Your point of contact may not always be the decision-maker; you don't want to pander to the wrong person. Pre-empt undesirable outcomes by familiarizing yourself as much as possible with your client and their business. For example, you may have been given a thorough brief, but if the person who prepared it is not responsible for making decisions, it could be all for nought.

The brief can change during a project, and it can change significantly without you being aware of it. The very nature of the creative process and your collaboration with the client can unearth ideas not previously considered. Be fluid and organic in your approach. When you feel the brief no longer reflects the direction of the project, be prepared to revise it with the client.

Take a time-out, and give yourself time to breathe and re-evaluate. Don't feel pressured to commit. Assess the situation and determine whether a realignment is in order. Better to backtrack a little now, because at the end you will just have further to backtrack.

Ask a lot of questions. The more you immerse yourself in the project, the more familiar you will become with the subject matter. Don't be afraid to keep asking questions if you feel they are important to the outcome of the project.

COMMUNICATION

For many freelancers, meeting the client face to face is not always possible, and you may run into complications if you haven't made provisions. Personally, I liaise with clients through email or Skype, but only when the brief and communication are solid. If the responses are short or not forthcoming, then I take it to the phone. Only then am I able to get a sense of what the client is about.

In my experience, we are getting lazy as communicators, trying to deal with all aspects of life — business and personal — via email and text messages. Some clients I've had have refused to speak with me by phone, while their written communication failed to inspire me with confidence.

If this happens to you, reflect on whether the project is worth taking on. If you have problems communicating before the project has even started, you will likely hit a brick wall when trying to get feedback on creative ideas or dealing with setbacks. I have on occasion "fired" clients because they were not pulling their weight, yet expected me to bust my gut. It doesn't work like that.

A true collaboration requires the commitment of at least two people: the designer and client.

TO CONCLUDE

There is no right or wrong answer to the question of whether to show all of your best ideas right away. Assess each client on their own terms and figure out what's best. Would the client be overwhelmed by too many choices, or would they welcome the variety? No one size fits all. On occasion, your experience or a hunch will tell you to focus on only one concept, with perhaps a few minor variations. The work period may be slow, and you have only one project on the go and are happy to spend the extra time on what may be a valuable repeat client.

Sometimes sticking your neck out and giving more than you are being paid to do is worthwhile, but that's a choice only you can make. Don't make it a habit, or your clients will come to expect that extra workload of you all the time: a quick path to freelance burn-out.

Being a good judge of character, understanding human interaction, being able to see past the here and now to pre-empt later problems, all of this helps you keep your sanity. Spend time learning and researching not only creative techniques but people, too. Your job and overall quality of life will improve as a result.

Graham Smith is a freelance logo designer, with ImJustCreative being his brand and identity. G's main motivation to wake up in the morning can be attributed to Helvetica, logos, typography, coffee, and Silly Putty. You'll also find G practicing the overt art of Social Media.

IV

CONTRACTS AND PRICING

21

FREELANCE CONTRACTS: DO'S AND DON'TS

by Robert Bowen

IN THE WORLD of freelancing, the entrepreneur has to take on a number of tasks for themselves that would normally be handled by a separate department at a bigger company. Most of these tasks are not part of the creative processes that freelance workers are used to, but rather are more tedious, left-brain paperwork. Right-brain creatives often shudder at the thought of these forays into linear domains. Such detail-ridden tasks would strain any freelancer who wears multiple hats, but they must be completed.

One such task is contracts. Drafting a contract that covers you, and doesn't just enumerate information, is more than important: it is a must. Freelancers do not have the benefit of a legal department dedicated to protecting their interests with a watertight contract. Nevertheless, a freelancer's contract must be comprehensive, concise, and clear. It should outline the scope of the job, scheduling demands, the expectations of both parties, and more.

In this chapter we help you identify the information that should be included in your contract and make sure you have a concrete agreement that leaves little chance of things getting out of hand — as can sometimes happen to those of us in the freelancing crowd.

These do's and don'ts will hopefully remove a lot of the headache and guesswork that comes with drafting a contract. By understanding the rationale behind various contractual elements, you will be able to better customize your contracts to fit the specific job you have been hired for.

THE BASICS

Include the basic information, obviously — the "who" and the "what" of the project. Who is contracting you to do what kind of work? This is standard stuff, included in every contract that defines the job as a whole. While this information is probably well known by both parties, put it in the contract anyway so that everyone is on the same page about their roles and responsibilities. Because it is such basic information, freelancers often overlook how important this section is for establishing the framework of the project.

DO'S AND DON'TS

K.I.S.S. Keep It Simple, Simon (your name may not be Simon, but it is nicer than the traditional "S" in the phrase.) Do be sure to clarify your role in the project from start to finish and describe exactly what it entails, so that the client doesn't try to put a hat on your head that you do not want to wear (for example, trying to make you switch from designing to providing tech support once the project has launched).

You know who you are and what your strengths are; don't leave room for the client to change your role in the project for his convenience. Be specific about what roles you are and are not willing to play.

TIME FRAME

This simply establishes the time that the project will take and the duration that the contract covers. Sometimes a freelancer has to leave time open after a project's completion to help integrate the product into the client's existing media stream. But not always. Determining that time frame at the beginning and formalizing it in the terms and conditions of the contract will ensure you are not taken advantage of.

DO'S AND DON'TS

Many people do not like deadlines, and some freelancers are no different. Whether you love or hate them, including deadlines in your contracts is important. Don't overlook this detail simply because of the pressure it may bring. Give yourself enough time to properly complete your tasks, while keeping the client's timetable in mind.

Being vague about how much time the contract covers will give your client room to find things for you to improve after the project has launched. Also, do be sure to include time frames on when the client needs to respond to your submissions with their questions and concerns, so that you are not endlessly strung along waiting to hear back on how to proceed.

DELIVERY DETAILS

Putting this in the contract further clarifies expectations at the outset. The client knows up front what the final product will be and how you will be delivering it to them. This frees you from having to guess later on things like what file types they can access, and it gives the client peace of mind knowing that you are both on the same page.

It also gives you an indication of the depth of the client's knowledge in this area of work and how well they will be able to work with the product once you hand it over. And being able to anticipate the client's need for assistance in accessing and integrating your product will help you formulate other parts of the contract.

DO'S AND DON'TS

Once again, keep it simple. Once you've assessed the client's needs, don't send them more files or file types than are needed to satisfy the project's requirements. Don't try to impress them with a Zip file full of extras that show how professional you are. This will overwhelm clients who are not design-savvy and encourages needless pestering. Keeping it simple will move your client happily along their way, not only giving you peace of mind from a job well done but freeing you from future distractions as you move on to your next client.

THE FINANCIALS

For most design work, billing by the job, rather than by the hour, is easier for everyone. You may have already come to an agreement on financial matters, but include them in the contract anyway for good measure. Just because you have an understanding about payment, the client could always conveniently "forget" the amount or change the terms.

DO'S AND DON'TS

Agree on an initial deposit (whatever seems fair) before doing any work, to protect both parties if either wants to back out. Make sure the client understands that this deposit protects them as well by committing you to the project and keeping you from being sidetracked by other clients. Also include a Cancellation Clause in the financial section of the contract. This isn't Santa's less famous brother; it actually protects you, the freelancer, in case your client backs out by stating the financial obligations of both parties should the project terminate before completion.

REVISIONS AND ALTERATIONS

You can also protect yourself by including a clause that states how many alterations and revisions to the product are covered by the fee. You can set the pricing for changes requested by the client that go beyond the number specified in the contract, thus preventing the client from abusing the privilege. Be clear that this is not a commentary on either party; by including this, you are not implying that the client will be hard to please or that you will need multiple attempts to get it right. It simply recognizes that we sometimes need time to fully process something before making a decision and that we should have the freedom to change our minds about whether an idea works or not once we actually see it in action.

DO'S AND DON'TS

Remember that professionalism should win out at all times, so don't let this part of the contract be any different. Yes, it can be aggravating when clients come back to you over and over with requests as a result of every whim that moves them, but do be reasonable. Don't punish all of your clients because of one that burned you in the past. And don't let pride keep you from accommodating a modest amount of revision by the client, even if they don't suit your taste. After all, the design may be yours, but they are paying you to create it for them.

THE FINE PRINT AND BOTTOM LINE

In the end, make sure the contract is professional and clear throughout, and be as detailed as possible in defining the roles of both parties in the project.

169

Robert Bowen is an emerging author, celebrated podcaster, and poet. He is the co-founder and imaginative co-contributor of the creative design and blogging duo at the Arbenting Blog and Dead Wings Designs.

22

WHAT'S IN A PRICE: GUIDELINES FOR PRICING WEB DESIGNS

by Thursday Bram

PRICING A WEBSITE design can seem impossible. A good website design can cost anywhere between thousands of dollars and under fifty dollars, depending on the type of site, how you build it, and a hundred other numbers. Those numbers can make it difficult to decide where the right price point for your own work is: how do you know what your work is worth when other designers' prices are all over the place?

All prices are not created equal: while it may seem to the lay person that all websites are similar, differences like the framework the site is built upon and the process the website designer uses can require drastically different prices. A website design that doesn't require you to do much more than design a new theme for WordPress probably shouldn't be priced the same way that an e-commerce site that expects to see plenty of traffic should be. It comes down to the question of what's in your price. In this article, we'll look at how four web designers set their prices — and how you can learn from their experiences.

THE BASICS OF PRICING

At the most basic, your prices must cover your expenses with hopefully a little extra left over, unless you have another source of income. The standard advice for determining your prices is to calculate what you need to live for a month — and then break that down to what you need to earn per hour. There are some nuances: it's rare for a web designer to have 40 hours of paying work every week. It's not impossible for a freelancer to have only 20 billable hours a week, especially when he's just starting out. The rest of the week may be spent marketing to new clients, handling paperwork, and other necessary tasks.

There's also the danger of underestimating your expenses when you decide on your rates. It's easy to miss one or two expenses, like health insurance, and wind up with prices that just won't work. It's important to build in a buffer when estimating the money that you need to bring in: your income needs to be able to cover savings, emergencies, and even price hikes on your standard expenses. These factors mean that the price range you find by estimating what you need to cover your expenses should actually be the bottom end of where you set your prices. Your own expenses are only a small part of what goes into the price you charge for a website design.

173

DECIDING BETWEEN PER PROJECT AND PER HOUR

One of the biggest decisions you have to make as a web designer is whether you'll charge per hour or per project. Most website designers think in terms of how many hours a project will take them to complete, which translates easily to charging by the hour. There are some other benefits, as well: an hourly rate makes it easy to revise an estimate if a client suddenly changes a project or needs an extra round of revisions.

SHOULD I CHARGE PER HOUR?

Mary-Frances Main is a web designer based in Colorado. She chooses to only work on an hourly basis. As Main says:

> We only quote per hour. Very very occasionally we will get a ballpark complete project cost, but rarely. We find that project bids very rarely end up in our favor. It's too difficult to adjust for design dilemmas or changes in direction or lack of organization from a client. We make up for not giving whole project bids by only charging updates with a base rate of a quarter of an hour.

The type of client Main usually works with is a big factor in her decision to work on an hourly basis. She prefers clients that need a web designer for the long haul — they need the web designer to handle updates, maintenance, and any adjustments the site needs. Because Main charges an hourly rate, she can comfortably handle those updates, while still making enough money to cover her needs.

Charging per hour makes sense if:

- Project requirements may change after you've already started working, It's hard to tell exactly how long a project will take.
- You're handling lots of small tasks or projects as they come up.
- Your client wants something beyond what you ordinarily offer.

SHOULD I CHARGE PER PROJECT?

While charging per hour makes sense for some web designers, it doesn't always make sense for everyone. There are drawbacks to pricing by the hour, as well. A client who doesn't really know what to expect in terms of the amount of work it takes to create a website can look at an hourly rate and quickly become concerned.

Having a rate of $100 per hour can scare off a client who thinks in terms of people working 40-hour workweeks. If you say that you can have the project done in three weeks, you can wind up with a client picturing a bill in the tens of thousands of dollars, no matter how large or small his project actually is. Giving a set rate for a whole project can eliminate that sort of pricing confusion.

Noel Green, a web designer based in New Mexico, takes a per project approach to pricing his work:

> While we have a per hour rate, we prefer to quote per project rather than per hour. After 8 years of doing this, we're quite good at knowing, approximately, how long a project is going to take us, so giving a client a 'flat fee' lets them feel more comfortable with the process.

Pricing per project has had other benefits for Green, as well. He's found that clients are less likely to add on to the original project if they know that they'll have to pay an hourly rate for any changes.

Charging per project makes sense if:

- You do this type of project often enough that you know how long it should take.
- Your client has a budget that doesn't allow for an open-ended number of hours.
- You want to offer a package deal, such as a website and hosting for a certain price.
- The project is relatively short and specific.

PRICE PER PROJECT AND PER HOUR

There is one other option, which Dixie Vogel, a web designer with more than 10 years of experience, uses. You can use per hour pricing in some situations and per project in others:

> *For larger projects, I price by project (after figuring out a time estimate to multiply against my base rate). I dislike time tracking and the feeling of rushing through work to keep my clients from being overcharged. I'm also frequently interrupted, which made tracking difficult. For small, limited scope projects, I do bill hourly as I tend to underestimate the time on simpler tasks and end up undercharging. Either way, however, I give my clients a range at the outset and stick very close to that.*

HOW LOW SHOULD I GO?

It can be tempting to price yourself below your competition, especially if you can bring in enough income to cover your expenses even at those lower prices. It seems like a lower price would get you more work and more clients. But it's a temptation you should avoid: not all clients assume that a low price means that a particular web designer is offering a deal. Instead, many prospective clients will think that there is a reason your prices are below those of other web designers with similar portfolios and skills. Maybe there's something wrong with your work or maybe you're a particularly slow worker — a low price could be more easily explained by a problem than by a web designer trying to set a price lower than his or her competition.

CHARGING FOR ALL THE TIME YOU SPEND

There's a more subtle version of this problem that can appear depending on just what you charge for. Many new web designers charge only for the time they spend actually creating and implementing a website. When Main first started designing websites, about nine years ago, she fell into this trap. Now, her prices cover a lot more:

> *We used to have entire email exchanges and design processes that went uncharged, we now log all of that time and charge for it accordingly.*

Beyond the actual time you spend on designing a website, you can and should bill your clients for the following:

- *Revisions:* It's rare for a client to like a design exactly the way you come up with it, but you can bill them for the time you spend revising your designs.
- *Education:* With some clients, you can spend hours going back and forth, educating them on what a website design actually includes. That is time you've spent on your project and it's time you can bill to your client.
- *Setup:* Some designers take care of setting up hosting, if not providing it entirely. The time it takes to get everything ready on the hosting end of things is an expense your client can cover.

EXPLAINING YOUR PRICES

There may be a client or two who questions your prices. It seems to happen more with clients that aren't familiar with the work necessary to create a website, but it can happen with a wide variety of client types. As long as you can explain your prices — and you remain firm on them — clients are typically willing to work with you. Green has had clients who tried to bargain and barter with him on his rates:

> *We didn't budge, so they chose someone else . . . the client who left because we wouldn't go down in price ended up coming back to us after the company they DID go with didn't deliver what they'd promised.*

When a prospective client wants to argue prices with you, it can be hard to stand firm, if only because you want the project even if it means dropping your rates a little. But there are a lot of reasons that a web designer can ask for high prices and get them:

- *You can complete a project significantly faster than an amateur.* It's cheaper to pay your hourly rate and get a good design quickly than to let a non-designer drag out the process for weeks or even months.

- *You do more than just design — you manage the project as a whole,* from creating a design to coordinating content.

- *You're a professional.* Your clients wouldn't ask a vendor to drop their prices.

It can be hard for a new web designer to price a project high enough, simply because of a lack of confidence. As you build your skills and gain confidence, it becomes easier to quote higher prices to clients without worrying that the price is too high. Stephanie Hobbs, a web designer based in South Carolina, has increased her prices along with her confidence:

> *When I started in 2003, my first paying website was $450 for five pages. Once I figured out a reasonable time estimate, I offered a four page site for $600. As my skill level has increased and I've raised my hourly rate, that number has gone to $800, $1000, and now $1200. My hourly rate started at $40 (I think, it might have been $50) and is now at $75. But I've raised my rates because I was very low to begin with because I didn't have confidence in myself.*

WHEN SHOULD I INCREASE MY PRICES?

What you charge today isn't necessarily what you should be charging a year from now. As you add to your skills, as well as your reputation, you'll not only be more valuable to your clients but you'll be able to demonstrate your worth with a larger portfolio of completed projects. You'll be able to increase your prices — and you should.

Vogel started freelancing at $25 per hour. She actually considers clients not complaining about prices a bad sign: "If no potential client complains, you're not charging enough."

As she raised her prices, Vogel would start quoting new projects at her higher rates, as well as informing her existing clients.

For any rate increases, I've always sent out notices to my clients explaining what I was doing beforehand and giving them all plenty of opportunity to opt out. I've never lost a single client raising my rates.

TIMING A PRICE INCREASE

Timing when you're going to announce your rate increase can be tricky, especially when you have existing clients or you've already offered an estimate for a new project. New clients are much easier to deal with: it's just a matter of quoting your new rate as you talk about new projects. With existing clients, however, you may find that they've gotten used to your old rates and aren't prepared to budget more for your services. There are a couple of times that it can be easier to announce those new rates:

- *The New Year:* With the end of the year approaching, you can simply send out a notice that your rates will be going up on the first of the year. The same approaches works with the beginning of a new month if you aren't prepared to wait until the end of the year.
- *New projects:* If your client brings you a new project, it can be an ideal time to make the switchover. You can explain that for future projects, you've increased your rates, which provides you and your client a chance to talk about the matter.
- *Contracts:* If you have a contract with your client to provide certain services, like maintenance, on a continuing basis, that contract should have an ending date. That date gives you an opportunity to renegotiate your rates.

Increasing your prices may not always be just a matter of making more money. If you want to be able to offer a discount on your work, as Hobbs does, having higher rates is necessary:

> *I do offer a 20% discount for people in my networking group, and a 30% discount to nonprofits (which is part of why I raised my rates from $1000 . . . I'm actually making closer to what I intended to make, since many of my clients are from my networking organization).*

PRICES IN THE WILD

All the information on how to set prices may not be enough to help you decide what is a reasonable price for your web design work. Actually seeing what other web designers charge is necessary to decide if your prices are comparable.

Mary-Frances Main charges $60 per hour for most web design work. For programming, her rate is $72 per hour and for Flash, her rate is $65 per hour.

Noel Green charges between $2,500 and $5,000 for a complete website, guaranteeing a four week turnaround on projects. Projects at the upper end of that range typically involve more complex features, such as shopping carts.

Dixie Vogel charges between $60 and $80 per hour for most web design work.

Stephanie Hobbs's rates start at $1,200 for a four-page website, add to her estimate for larger projects and sites with extra features, like Flash.

These prices differ due to factors like the designer's location, their experience, and even the type of clients they prefer to work with. But, in each case, the web designer in question has thought through not only what he or she needs to earn but how comparable those prices are to other designers and where the prices can be increased.

Thursday Bram is a full-time freelancer who has been working on her own for more than seven years. She writes about the business side of freelancing and maintains her own website.

23

QUALITY-PRICE RATIO IN WEB DESIGN

by Jeff Gardner

I'M ABOUT TO *make a bold statement.* The quality of a design and the monetary cost of producing or procuring that design have absolutely no relationship whatsoever. It's a bitter pill to swallow, I know. Many of you are crying foul at this very moment, but hear me out. I'll explain my radical position — and hopefully give you a few pointers about how to more effectively price and position your design business in this brave new, and uncorrelated, world.

Quality-Price Ratio (or QPR) is a concept that is used extensively in the wine trade. In its essence it's nothing more than a measure of perceived value, of the enjoyment you receive weighed against the price you have to pay. Do you feel that the benefit you gained was worth the price you've paid? If you don't, then the product or service has a low QPR. On the other hand, if you feel like you got away with highway robbery then the product or service has a very high QPR. I'll spare you the metaphysical comparisons between wine and design beyond this one important point: There is no correlation between price and quality when discussing wine or design.

THE ASSUMPTIONS

The following sections address a few common assumptions about design and value.

GOOD DESIGN IS SUBJECTIVE

While most good design shares many of the same basic characteristics, beyond a certain point the perceived value of all design is subjective. What appeals to me may not appeal to you; in fact, you could go so far as to say that you hate it. But, if you were being honest (and the work in question was in fact well done) you would have to admit that it was, at the very least, well put together.

GOOD DESIGN IS CHEAP

Don't misunderstand me. I'm not saying that good design should be cheap or that it always is cheap. I'm just saying that, these days, good design can be found very inexpensively. Think 99designs, Graphic Leftovers, and even some of the more reputable stock agencies. These services are extraordinarily popular because they bring good design to people on a budget. These services can also be extraordinarily difficult to compete against.

GOOD DESIGN HAS NO CORRELATION WITH PRICE

From the client's point of view, the QPR of design falls into four, and only four, categories. Listed from lowest QPR to highest:

1. *Bad design that's expensive.* As a client, you do not want to be here — it's a world of pain.

2. *Bad design that's cheap.* This type of design, I think we'll all agree, has a fairly low QPR because, well, it still sucks even though you paid very little for it.

3. *Good design that's expensive.* This is a tough one. You've gotten a great product, but you've paid a hefty price. You normally just tell yourself that you did the right thing because everyone knows, "you get what you pay for."

4. *Good design that's cheap.* This category has the highest QPR because you are getting a great product for a small price! Who doesn't want to be here?

Your clients are clearly looking for that magic fourth category, while you're trying to get them closer to the third. This is what makes selling design so difficult — your interests and the client's interests are clearly at odds.

GOOD DESIGN IS ABOUT ATTITUDE

A little attitude and a little cockiness never hurt anyone. I would argue that those two qualities have actually helped more businesses than they've harmed.

Why? Because being confident in your product or service is infectious. If you believe strongly in the value and the worth of what you're selling, your clients are going to see that, and respond in kind.

GOOD DESIGN IS ABOUT BRANDING

Brand is all about good will. Having high brand equity is nothing more than having a stockpile of good emotions and good response reactions from consumers. What does this have to do with good design? It doesn't, other than the fact that consumers will give the benefit of the doubt to a design that has a strong brand behind it. They may not know what good design is, but if they respect your name, chances are they will respect your design.

PRICING STRATEGIES

Let's face it, deciding how to price your creative services is hard. You are, in essence, trying to attach a discrete number to your creative acumen, which makes it seem very much like you are bragging if you charge a lot or like you have no backbone if you charge too little. But it is imperative that you get beyond these feelings. Design, and good design especially, is a very scarce resource and, as such, should be priced accordingly. But how to go about arriving at a number?

A note about premium services: I once heard about a wedding photographer (who charged average prices) that wanted to work less. So, she figured that if she just began raising her prices there would simply be less interest from clients. First she bumped up to $3,000 a weekend, then $4,000, then $5,000. To her astonishment, she actually began receiving more requests from clients. The clients figured that if she was charging such a high sum, she must be really good. Truth being told, she hadn't gotten any better, she'd always been a good photographer — but the higher price led her potential clients to believe this and, in the end, they were never disappointed. Finally this photographer raised her prices to $20,000 per weekend, essentially pricing herself above what almost anyone could afford. Her potential clients then began offering to fly her to remote locations around the world just for the chance to have her shoot their exotic weddings.

I think you get my point. The old economic adage that higher price correlates to lower demand doesn't always hold true, and this is especially true of luxury goods. Design is a premium service. A luxury good. It is certainly not necessary to run a business (just take a look at all the used car dealers of the world for confirmation), but results in a definite advantage to the businesses who value good design. Don't be surprised to find that design and the pricing of design follows a slightly paradoxical pricing relationship.

This little story also illustrates how important market positioning is to luxury goods. You'd be a fool to try and compete on price with sites like 99designs, so don't try. Compete on completeness, your creative vision, and your customer service.

With our new assumptions and the idea that design is a luxury good, let's take a look at a few tips to help you formulate a sensible price for your design services.

DON'T CHARGE PER HOUR

Design, or any other creative endeavor, should never be charged hourly. I know, it's an industry standard method, but I whole-heartedly disagree with it — and here's why.

Charging hourly works fantastically for things like stamping exhaust pipes or writing legal briefs — any type of job that is characterized by taking inputs and transforming those inputs using a specific process. It's easy to see the direct correlation between hours and number of exhaust pipes or legal briefs.

On the other hand, with creative pursuits, and design in particular, there is often no time correlation whatsoever. Sometimes you get that spark and a project takes two hours, sometimes you have to batter yourself for days before you feel that you have something remotely resembling a decent design. Should the client in the first instance have to pay nearly nothing for their design while the client in the second pays through the teeth?

Hourly rates are unfair to both the designer and the client. Well then, I can hear you asking, if not hourly, how are you supposed to figure out how to charge?

THE COST OF DOING BUSINESS

The first step in coming to a fair and reasonable valuation of your services is to take a look at your cost of doing business. Cost of business is simply everything that it takes for you to operate. The cost of your computer, the cost of all the software that you use, if you rent office space, the cost of your office space. Think of every single thing that you use on a daily basis to get your work done and write them all down. This is your cost of doing business (I find it easiest if it's written in monthly terms), and you should revisit and revise this number at least once a year. To estimate a per project break-even figure, you can divide your monthly cost of doing business by your average number of projects completed in a month and you will have an average baseline project cost.

Your cost of doing business serves as a baseline to your pricing equation. This, by the way, doesn't mean that the average baseline project cost is the lowest price you can ever charge for a project, but, it should, instead, serve as a guidepost to help you maintain profitability.

THE CREATIVITY COEFFICIENT

Let's not mince words, creativity is hard work. It's not rote production, transforming inputs using a standard process. Design, as with all creative pursuits, is all about creating something from nothing; and because of this, creative work demands its own pricing methods.

Price = Creativity Coefficient × Cost of doing business

The creativity coefficient is nothing more than a multiplier that you apply to your base cost of doing business. This coefficient (or multiplier) gives the designer a measure of control to help match the prices they charge with the difficulty and involvement of the projects they work on. The creativity coefficient should be based upon three things:

- *Difficulty.* If the project is difficult or very involved, charge more. This should be clear at this point. If you're producing one tri-fold brochure your multiplier may be as low as 1.20; on the other hand if you are completely rebranding and redesigning a medium to large company's image, your creativity coefficient may go as high as 10 or 15.
- *Brand strength.* Simply put, if you have a strong brand behind you, charge more. At first glance this may seem unfair but, in reality, it is the simplest and most effective way to separate potential clients into the two groups that matter: the ones that just want to work with you because of your name, but are going to be a major headache (especially over price), and the ones that recognize the value that your brand brings and are willing to pay for that value.
- *Individuality.* If the client is coming to you because you specialize in a certain type of design or in a specific medium and there is no one else out there that can competently perform the work, charge more. Niche work is important and there is value in being different; especially in today's hyper-homogenized world, clients that come looking for something different will be expecting to pay premium prices for something that they cannot get anywhere else.

The creativity coefficient gives designers a simple and effective way to try and wrangle concrete numbers around the value of creativity. And because you are starting with a baseline amount that reflects your actual cost of doing business you are ensuring that your business will stay profitable.

THE TAKE-AWAY

Finding a balance in the way that you price your designs isn't just about economics and finding the highest number that you can get away with. These guidelines are just that, guidelines. Hopefully they have given you a new, and inspiring, light in which to view your services and the value of those services, but in the end, it comes down to feeling that you are providing a valuable service to your clients and that you are being fairly paid for those services.

Jeff Gardner is a business nerd who loves spreadsheets, graphs, and helping companies figure out how to perform better. He also enjoys writing, photography, and being outside.

Index